This Book Belongs to:

Turkey with Maple Glaze
(page 31)

Very Merry Christmas Cookbook

Over 185 tried & true recipes, scrumptious menu ideas & clever how-to's for a magical Christmas!

Oxmoor House®

Very Merry Christmas Cookbook

©2007 by Gooseberry Patch
600 London Road, Delaware, Ohio 43015,
www.gooseberrypatch.com
©2007 by Oxmoor House, Inc.
Book Division of Southern Progress Corporation
P. O. Box 2262, Birmingham, Alabama 35201-2262

Hardcover ISBN-13: 978-0-8487-3180-9
Hardcover ISBN-10: 0-8487-3180-8
Softcover ISBN-13: 978-0-8487-3181-6
Softcover ISBN-10: 0-8487-3181-6
Library of Congress Control Number: 2006908799
Printed in the United States of America
First Printing 2007

Oxmoor House, Inc.
Editor in Chief: Nancy Fitzpatrick Wyatt
Executive Editor: Susan Carlisle Payne
Art Director: Keith McPherson
Managing Editor: Allison Long Lowery

Gooseberry Patch Very Merry Christmas Cookbook
Editor: Kelly Hooper Troiano
Copy Editor: Donna Baldone
Editorial Assistants: Amelia Heying, Rachel Quinlivan
Photography Director: Jim Bathie
Senior Photo Stylist: Kay E. Clarke
Associate Photo Stylist: Katherine G. Eckert
Director, Test Kitchens: Elizabeth Tyler Austin
Assistant Director, Test Kitchens: Julie Christopher
Food Stylist: Kelley Self Wilton
Test Kitchens Professionals: Kathleen Royal Phillips,
    Catherine Crowell Steele, Ashley T. Strickland
Director of Production: Laura Lockhart
Production Manager: Theresa Beste-Farley
Production Assistant: Faye Porter Bonner

Contributors
Designer: Amy R. Bickell
Indexer: Mary Ann Laurens
Interns: Amy Edgerton, Carol Corbin
Food Stylists: Ana Price Kelly, Debby Maugans
Test Kitchens Professionals: Jane Chambliss, Kate Wheeler, R.D.
Photographer: Lee Harrelson
Photo Stylist: Leigh Anne Montgomery

For books: To order additional publications, call 1-800-765-6400.
For more books to enrich your life, visit oxmoorhouse.com

Cover: Chocolate Pecan Pie (page 39)

Contents

Chocolate-
Macadamia Pie
(page 27)

Dear Friend,

Christmas is the most festive time of year...and what better way to celebrate this magical season than gathering with the ones you hold dear. Whether you're enjoying a white Christmas or just dreaming of one, let the joy of the season begin as you thumb through the pages of our newest book, *Gooseberry Patch Very Merry Christmas Cookbook*.

You'll be inspired as you look over the selection of over 185 tried & true mouthwatering recipes. This year you're invited to peek inside the kitchen files of our family at Gooseberry Patch. Staff members collected their holiday favorites and heartfelt memories to share with you. In addition, our friends from across the country not only share their favorite recipes but their treasured memories & traditions as well. We promise you'll be inspired to create your own ideas for holiday cooking as you read through these heartwarming recollections.

Don't miss our special section on Goodies for Giving starting on page 134. Not only will you have an abundance of yummy gifts to share with the special people in your life, but we include clever ideas for packaging and whimsical gift tags you can photocopy onto card stock to accompany them. Meal planning will be a cinch with help from the Merry Christmas Menu (page 18) and the 12 Days of Christmas Menus (page 148). Next be sure to check out our helpful holiday how-to's for enjoying all the merriment with the greatest of ease. A special planner section provides entertaining hints and handy calendars to organize the must-do's during the holiday months. And be sure to look for the journal-type pages that begin on page 150 where you can jot down menu plans, the highlights of the season and everyone's favorite dish.

This year let our *Very Merry Christmas Cookbook* add magic to your season as you usher in the holidays with family & friends.

Wishing you all the joys of Christmas!

Vickie & JoAnn

Country Breakfast
Sandwich (page 12)

Gooseberry Patch Family

holiday favorites

Vickie likes to serve savory Black-Eyed Pea Dip to her

family & friends during the holidays while JoAnn bakes a casserole of

Country Breakfast Sandwiches to kick off her big holiday. Take a peek at

these and other time-honored recipes and memories that your friends at

Gooseberry Patch like to share throughout the season.

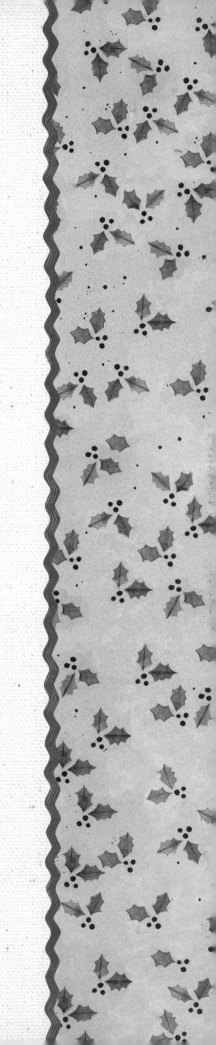

Black-Eyed Pea Dip

Black-Eyed Pea Dip

16-oz. can black-eyed peas, rinsed,
   drained and divided
3 green onions, chopped
½ c. sour cream
1 t. garlic salt

½ c. salsa
4 slices bacon, crisply cooked and
   crumbled
Tortilla, corn or bagel chips

Set aside ⅓ cup peas. Place remaining peas in an electric blender and process until smooth. Add onions, sour cream and garlic salt to blender; process until smooth. Transfer to a bowl and stir in salsa, bacon and reserved peas. Serve with chips. Serves 8.

Aunt Ruthie's Breakfast Casserole

Softened butter or margarine
16 slices bread, crusts removed
1 lb. shaved deli ham
4 c. (1 lb.) shredded Cheddar cheese
4 oz. grated Parmesan cheese
2 (4.5-oz.) cans sliced mushrooms,
   drained

4 eggs, lightly beaten
½ t. dry mustard
3 c. milk
½ t. salt
¼ t. pepper
¼ t. onion salt
½ c. corn flake crumbs

Butter one side of each bread slice. Layer one-third of bread, butter side up, in a greased 13"x9" baking dish. Layer a third each of ham, cheeses and mushrooms; repeat layers twice. Stir together eggs, mustard, milk, salt, pepper and onion salt; pour over mixture in dish. Cover and chill overnight in the refrigerator.

Let stand at room temperature 30 minutes before baking. Sprinkle casserole with corn flake crumbs. Bake, uncovered, at 350 degrees for 45 minutes. Let cool 10 minutes before serving. Serves 8 to 10.

AS A KID, IT JUST WOULDN'T HAVE BEEN CHRISTMAS WITHOUT CHOCOLATE FUDGE! My mom had only one cookbook and one particular fudge recipe we always made together. We laughed and we agonized over that fudge! We didn't have a candy thermometer, so it was my responsibility to make sure it reached the "soft ball" stage. I prepared several cups of icy cold water (anticipating several "tests"). Once the fudge started boiling, I spooned a small amount of the creamy confection into the first cup...and I repeated the process as many times as necessary (sometimes a half dozen or more!) until a soft ball of fudge could be formed. There were times when the anticipation was so great I cut the "soft ball" process short and, as a result, we poured the "fudge" over ice cream or pulled it like taffy or caramel. It was never wasted, though. The best part...I always got the pan and spoon to "clean up" at the end. Thanks for all the sweet memories, Mom!

VICKIE
CO-FOUNDER

Country Breakfast Sandwiches

(pictured on page 8)

"For a change, why not try pancakes or toasted bagels in place of the toast in these breakfast sandwiches? Whichever you choose, it'll be so scrumptious!"

Jo Ann
Co-Founder

3 T. butter or margarine, divided
1 Granny Smith apple, peeled, cored and thinly sliced
2 slices whole-wheat bread, toasted

3 links pork sausage, halved lengthwise and browned
¼ c. maple syrup, warmed

Heat 2 tablespoons butter in a skillet over low heat. Add apple; sauté until tender and golden, turning often.

Spread toasted bread with remaining butter; top each slice with sausages, apple slices and syrup. Serves 2.

My Favorite One-Pot Meal

"Curry powder, raisins and chopped apple make this chicken dish just a little different."

Liz Plotnick-Snay
Chief Operating Officer

2 onions, diced
¼ c. oil, divided
2½ to 3 lbs. boneless, skinless chicken breasts
14½-oz. can diced tomatoes
½ c. white wine or chicken broth
1 T. curry powder
¼ t. garlic powder

¼ t. dried thyme
¼ t. ground nutmeg
1 apple, peeled, cored and cubed
¼ c. raisins
3 T. whipping cream
½ t. lemon juice
2 c. cooked rice

Sauté onions in 2 tablespoons oil in a large skillet over medium heat; remove onions and set aside.

Add remaining oil and chicken to skillet; cook chicken until golden. Return onions to skillet; add tomatoes, wine and next 4 ingredients, stirring well. Reduce heat, cover and simmer for 20 minutes.

Add apple, raisins and cream to skillet; simmer over low heat 6 to 8 more minutes. Stir in lemon juice. Serve over cooked rice. Serves 3 to 4.

ONE CHRISTMAS, MY MOM HAD A SPECIAL SURPRISE FOR ME. I was excited because it was rare that we did anything without at least one of my five brothers & sisters tagging along. To a 7 year-old, the drive from rural New Jersey to New York City was very long but it was well worth it. We were setting out alone to see...the Rockettes! What I remember about that day are the twinkling lights at Radio City Music Hall, the hustle & bustle on the street and my small hand held warm and tight in Mom's. Everything seemed to be touched with magic. We waited in line, then in our scratchy seats and finally, they took the stage. I was in heaven! The costumes were fantastic and music filled the entire hall. Best of all, my mom's face mirrored my own delight.

Jo Ann
Co-Founder

Hearty Winter Pork Stew

Hearty Winter Pork Stew

2 lbs. boneless pork loin, cubed
1 t. salt, divided
1 t. pepper, divided
1 T. olive oil
2 c. sliced parsnips
1½ c. sliced carrots
1 small butternut squash, peeled and cubed
½ c. chopped onion
4 c. chicken broth
¼ c. all-purpose flour
3 T. butter or margarine, softened

Sprinkle pork with ½ teaspoon each of salt and pepper. Brown pork in hot oil in a large skillet over medium-high heat.

Layer pork and vegetables in a *5-quart slow cooker*. Pour broth over vegetables. Sprinkle with remaining ½ teaspoon each of salt and pepper. Cover and cook on LOW setting 6 hours.

Stir together flour and butter in a small bowl; gently stir into stew one tablespoon at a time. Increase heat to HIGH setting; cover and cook 30 minutes until thickened, stirring occasionally. Serves 4 to 6.

"This stew's nutritious…and filling! Try other varieties of winter squash instead of butternut…they're all delicious!"

JENNIE GIST
BOOK EDITOR

Mexicali Chicken

4 cooked chicken breasts, shredded
12-oz. jar salsa
2 c. shredded colby-Jack cheese

8-oz. pkg. noodles
1 T. butter or margarine
1 t. Italian seasoning

Place shredded chicken and salsa in a large skillet over medium heat; simmer for 10 minutes or until thoroughly heated. Sprinkle with cheese; cover and continue simmering until cheese is melted.

Meanwhile, cook noodles according to package directions; drain. Stir in butter and seasoning. Evenly spoon chicken mixture over individual servings of noodles. Serves 6 to 8.

Candied Fruitcake

3 (7½-oz.) pkgs. pitted dates, chopped
16-oz. pkg. candied pineapple, chopped
16-oz. pkg. whole red candied cherries
2 c. all-purpose flour

2 t. baking powder
½ t. salt
4 eggs, beaten
1 c. sugar
2 (16-oz.) pkgs. pecan halves

Combine dates, pineapple and cherries in a large bowl. Stir together flour, baking powder and salt in a second bowl; add fruit mixture. Mix well with hands; separate pieces so that all are well coated.

In another bowl, blend eggs with a hand mixer until frothy; gradually blend in sugar. Add to fruit mixture; mix well with a large spoon. Add pecans; mix with hands until evenly distributed and coated with batter.

Grease 2 (9") springform pans or 2 (9"x5") loaf pans; line with parchment paper cut to fit, then grease paper. Spread mixture in pans; press mixture down with hands; rearrange pieces of fruit and nuts as necessary to fill up any empty spaces. Bake at 275 degrees for 1¼ to 1½ hours; tops will look dry when done. Remove from oven; cool 5 minutes on wire racks. Turn out onto wire racks, carefully peel off paper and cool thoroughly. Store loosely wrapped. Makes 2 cakes.

BACK IN THE 1960s, my mom used to make lots of these fruitcakes every Christmas to send as gifts to relatives. I can still remember going to the Kresge's dimestore with her to buy the candied fruit at the candy counter. We all love this fruitcake...it's all candied fruit, pecans and just enough batter to hold it together.

JENNIE GIST
BOOK EDITOR

Espresso Biscotti

Espresso Biscotti

¼ c. ground espresso
2 T. coffee-flavored liqueur or double-
    strength brewed coffee
½ c. butter or margarine, softened
¾ c. sugar

2 eggs
2 c. plus 2 T. all-purpose flour
1½ t. baking powder
¼ t. salt
⅔ c. slivered almonds, toasted

Place espresso in a small microwave-safe bowl. Add liqueur and microwave on HIGH (100%) for 10 to 15 seconds to steep; set aside.

Beat butter and sugar at medium speed with an electric mixer until light and fluffy. Add eggs, one at a time, beating until blended; stir in coffee mixture. Combine flour, baking powder and salt; add to butter mixture, stirring until blended. Fold in nuts. Divide dough in half.

On a greased baking sheet, shape dough into two 13"x1½"x½" rectangles, spacing them about 2 inches apart. Bake at 325 degrees for 20 to 25 minutes or until golden. Remove to a wire rack; let cool 5 minutes.

Place biscotti on a cutting board; using a serrated knife, cut biscotti diagonally into ½-inch-thick slices. Place slices upright on baking sheet ½ inch apart and bake 10 more minutes. Let cool on rack. Store in a tightly covered container. Makes 2 dozen.

"Crunchy coffee dippers! Make them even better by stirring some white chocolate chips into the dough, then drizzle finished cookies with melted dark chocolate."

STACIE MICKLEY
BOOK ASSISTANT

Frosted Turtle Cookies

1½ c. all-purpose flour
¼ t. baking soda
¼ t. salt
½ c. butter, softened
½ c. brown sugar, packed

1 egg
1 egg, separated
¼ t. vanilla extract
½ lb. pecan halves (80 halves)

Stir together flour, soda and salt. Beat butter at medium speed with an electric mixer until creamy; gradually add sugar, beating well. Add egg and egg yolk, beating well. Gradually add flour mixture, mixing well. Stir in vanilla. (Dough will be soft.) Cover and chill 30 minutes. Arrange pecan halves in groups of five on greased baking sheets to resemble head and legs of a turtle.

Shape dough into 1½-inch balls, using a rounded teaspoonful of dough for each so tips of nuts will show when cookies are baked. Dip bottom of dough into unbeaten egg white and press lightly onto nuts; flatten tops slightly.

Bake at 350 degrees for 12 to 14 minutes. (Do not overbake.) Cool completely on wire racks. Generously spread frosting on top of cookies. Makes 16.

Chocolate Frosting

3 T. butter, softened
1½ c. powdered sugar, sifted

6 T. baking cocoa
¼ c. whipping cream

Beat butter in a small mixing bowl at medium speed with an electric mixer until creamy. Gradually add sugar, cocoa and whipping cream, beating until smooth. Makes 1⅛ cups.

Snow Ice Cream

1 c. heavy cream
Sugar to taste

Vanilla extract to taste
4 c. clean snow

Beat cream at high speed with an electric mixer until stiff peaks form; add sugar and vanilla to taste. Fold in snow, blending well. Eat immediately or freeze until ice cream has hardened. Serves 4 to 6.

"My great-grandma's recipe…these cookies have been at all of our holiday family gatherings since the 1940s."

TAMI BOWMAN
MANAGING EDITOR

"Snow Ice Cream is a treat our family looks forward to after the very first snowfall...our kids love how the snow 'magically' turns into ice cream!"

MARY MURRAY
SENIOR BOOK EDITOR

Frosted Turtle
Cookies

Holiday Beef Tenderloin (page 23),
Asparagus with Mushrooms and
Bacon (page 24) and Blue Cheese and
Cheddar Potato Gratin (page 23)

Merry Christmas menu

Gather your family around the table for a memorable feast filled with heart-warming tradition, good food and lasting memories…it's easy with such savory selections as beef tenderloin and cheesy potatoes and such grand finales as Quick Italian Cream Cake and Chocolate-Macadamia Pie!

Menu for 8

Cheery Cheese Ring

Sweet Potato-Peanut Soup

Spinach-and-Cranberry Salad

Holiday Beef Tenderloin

Blue Cheese and Cheddar Potato Gratin

Asparagus with Mushrooms and Bacon

Quick Italian Cream Cake

Chocolate-Macadamia Pie

Cheery Cheese Ring

For an extra-special treat, look for vintage cake molds in festive shapes at flea markets and antique shops in which to shape this cheese spread. Serve strawberry preserves on the side, if you'd like.

16 oz. sharp Cheddar cheese, finely grated
4 oz. cream cheese, softened
¼ c. mayonnaise
1 onion, minced

1 c. chopped walnuts
¼ t. garlic powder
⅛ t. chili powder
⅛ t. hot pepper sauce
1 c. strawberry preserves

Combine all ingredients except strawberry preserves in a large bowl; mix well. Scoop mixture onto a serving platter; wet your hands and shape into a ring. Pour strawberry preserves into the center. Serve with assorted crackers. Serves 12.

Sweet Potato-Peanut Soup

1 T. butter
½ large sweet onion, chopped
1 small celery rib, diced
2 carrots, sliced
¼ t. ground red pepper
1½ lbs. sweet potatoes, peeled and cubed

3¼ c. chicken broth
1 c. half-and-half
½ c. creamy peanut butter
Nutmeg-Molasses Cream
Chopped toasted peanuts

Melt butter in a large Dutch oven; add onion and next 3 ingredients and sauté over medium heat 3 minutes. Add sweet potato cubes and chicken broth; cook over medium heat 30 minutes, stirring occasionally.

Process mixture, in batches, in an electric blender or food processor until smooth. Return mixture to Dutch oven; whisk in half-and-half and peanut butter. Reduce heat to low and simmer 15 minutes, stirring often. Serve with Nutmeg-Molasses Cream and chopped toasted peanuts. Serves 8.

Nutmeg-Molasses Cream

1 c. whipping cream
3 T. molasses

¼ t. ground nutmeg

Beat whipping cream at medium speed with an electric mixer until soft peaks form; gradually beat in molasses and nutmeg. Chill until ready to serve. Makes about 2 cups.

Ask a few questions to stir Christmas dinner conversation.

What's a favorite holiday memory? Does anyone have a Christmas wish this year? What about a New Year's wish? Asking questions is a nice way to share sweet memories and catch up with friends & family during this special time of year.

Sweet Potato-
Peanut Soup

Spinach-and-
Cranberry Salad

Get a head start on dinner by preparing and chilling the ingredients for the salad ahead. Toss the salad with the dressing right before serving.

Spinach-and-Cranberry Salad

2 T. butter or margarine
1½ c. coarsely chopped pecans
1 t. salt
1 t. freshly ground pepper
2 (6-oz.) pkgs. fresh baby spinach

6 slices bacon, crisply cooked and
    crumbled
1 c. dried cranberries
2 eggs, hard-cooked and chopped
Warm Chutney Dressing

Melt butter in a nonstick skillet over medium-high heat; add pecans and cook, stirring constantly, 2 minutes or until toasted. Remove from heat; add salt and pepper, tossing to coat. Drain pecans on paper towels.

Toss together pecans, spinach, bacon, cranberries and eggs. Drizzle with Warm Chutney Dressing, gently tossing to coat. Serve immediately. Serves 8.

Warm Chutney Dressing

6 T. balsamic vinegar
⅓ c. bottled mango chutney
2 T. Dijon mustard

2 T. honey
2 cloves garlic, minced
¼ c. olive oil

Cook first 5 ingredients in a saucepan over medium heat, stirring constantly, 3 minutes. Stir in olive oil, blending well; cook one minute. Makes one cup.

Holiday Beef Tenderloin

(pictured on page 18)

1 T. salt
1½ t. onion powder
1½ t. garlic powder
1½ t. black pepper
1 t. ground red pepper
½ t. ground cumin

½ t. ground nutmeg
5-lb. beef tenderloin, trimmed
¼ c. olive oil
Garnishes: fresh rosemary sprigs,
    fresh sage sprigs

Combine first 7 ingredients in a small bowl.

Rub tenderloin with oil; coat with spice mixture. Place in a large roasting pan; cover and chill 8 hours.

Bake at 500 degrees for 15 minutes or until browned. Lower temperature to 375 degrees; bake 20 more minutes or to desired degree of doneness. Let stand 10 minutes; then slice and serve with horseradish mayonnaise. Garnish, if desired. Serves 8.

Nutmeg delivers a hint of sweetness that balances the spiciness from the black and red peppers in this tenderloin. Look for horseradish mayonnaise on the condiment aisle of your local supermarket.

Blue Cheese and Cheddar Potato Gratin

(pictured on page 18)

¼ c. butter or margarine
¼ c. all-purpose flour
1 c. whipping cream
1 c. milk
½ t. salt
½ t. ground white pepper
¼ t. ground nutmeg
½ c. crumbled blue cheese
2 t. minced garlic

1 c. thinly sliced onion, separated into
    rings
2 lbs. red potatoes, peeled and thinly
    sliced
9-oz. pkg. frozen artichoke hearts,
    thawed and drained
1 c. (4 oz.) shredded white Cheddar
    cheese

Melt butter in a heavy saucepan over low heat; add flour, stirring until smooth. Cook, stirring constantly, one minute. Gradually add cream and milk and cook over medium heat, stirring constantly, until mixture is thickened and bubbly. Stir in salt, pepper and nutmeg.

Sprinkle blue cheese and garlic in a lightly greased 13"x9" baking dish. Arrange half of onion rings over blue cheese and garlic; top with half of potato slices. Arrange artichoke hearts over potato slices. Pour half of sauce mixture over artichoke hearts. Repeat layers with remaining onion, potato slices and sauce mixture. Bake, covered, at 350 degrees for one hour. Sprinkle evenly with Cheddar cheese. Bake, uncovered, 15 more minutes or until potatoes are tender. Let stand 10 minutes before serving. Serves 10.

Asparagus with Mushrooms and Bacon

(pictured on page 18)

2 lbs. fresh asparagus
8 slices bacon
3 c. sliced shiitake mushrooms
  (about 7 oz.)

¼ c. chopped shallots
⅛ to ¼ t. dried crushed red pepper
½ t. freshly ground black pepper
¼ t. salt

Snap off and discard tough ends of asparagus. Cut asparagus into pieces. Cook in boiling salted water to cover in a Dutch oven over medium-high heat for 4 minutes; drain. Plunge into ice water to stop the cooking process; drain and set aside.

Cook bacon in a large skillet over medium-low heat until crisp; remove bacon and drain on paper towels, reserving 1½ tablespoons drippings in skillet. Discard remaining drippings. Crumble bacon.

Sauté mushrooms and shallots in hot drippings over medium-high heat 5 minutes or until shallots are tender. Add asparagus and crushed red pepper; sauté one to 2 minutes or until thoroughly heated. Stir in crumbled bacon, pepper and salt. Serves 8.

Quick Italian Cream Cake

18¼-oz. pkg. white cake mix with
  pudding
3 eggs
1¼ c. buttermilk
¼ c. vegetable oil

3½-oz. can flaked coconut
⅔ c. chopped pecans, toasted
3 T. rum (optional)
Cream Cheese Frosting
Garnish: pecan halves

Beat first 4 ingredients at medium speed with an electric mixer 2 minutes. Stir in coconut and pecans. Pour batter into 3 greased and floured 9" round cake pans.

Bake at 350 degrees for 15 to 17 minutes or until a wooden toothpick inserted in center comes out clean. Cool in pans on wire racks 10 minutes. Remove from pans and cool completely on wire racks. Sprinkle cake layers evenly with rum, if desired; let stand 10 minutes.

Spread Cream Cheese Frosting between layers and on top and sides of cake. Garnish, if desired. Chill 2 hours before slicing. Serves 12.

Cream Cheese Frosting

1½ pkgs. (12 oz.) cream cheese,
  softened
¾ c. butter or margarine, softened

6 c. powdered sugar
1 c. chopped pecans, toasted
2 t. vanilla extract

Beat cream cheese and butter at medium speed with an electric mixer until smooth. Gradually add powdered sugar, beating until light and fluffy. Stir in pecans and vanilla. Makes 4 cups.

Chocolate-
Macadamia Pie

Chocolate-Macadamia Pie

4 eggs, lightly beaten
¾ c. light corn syrup
½ c. brown sugar, packed
¼ c. butter or margarine, melted
2 t. Kahlúa or other coffee-flavored
   liqueur

2 t. vanilla extract
1 c. semi-sweet chocolate chips
7-oz. jar macadamia nuts
1 unbaked 9" pastry shell
Coffee Cream
¼ c. shaved semi-sweet chocolate

This luscious mocha-flavored pie is just as good with pecans as with macadamia nuts, if you'd like to substitute.

Combine first 6 ingredients in a medium bowl; stir well. Stir in chocolate chips and nuts.

Pour into pastry shell; bake at 425 degrees for 10 minutes. Reduce oven temperature to 350 degrees and bake 30 more minutes or until set. (Cover edges of pastry with strips of aluminum foil to prevent excessive browning, if necessary.) Cool completely on a wire rack; cover and chill thoroughly.

To serve, dollop each serving with Coffee Cream and sprinkle with shaved chocolate. Serves 8.

Coffee Cream

1 c. whipping cream
2 T. powdered sugar

2 T. Kahlúa or other coffee-flavored
   liqueur

Combine all ingredients in a large bowl; beat at high speed with an electric mixer until stiff peaks form. Makes 2 cups.

WE SPENT EVERY CHRISTMAS AT GRANDMA'S. Her table was filled with great Italian dishes, good conversation and close relatives. One year, as we sat down to dinner, Grandma handed me a pen and told me to write my name on her linen tablecloth! She insisted I sign and pass the pen along to the others. The following Christmas Eve, I noticed she had embroidered all our names on that cloth with brightly colored thread. Even though several family members were not there that year, their names reminded us of many good times. Each of us will forever have a special place at our family dinner table. Years have gone by, yet we use that same tablecloth. This year, the tablecloth is well over 20 years old and we still each have our "special" place at the table!

DENISE GIDARO
BADEN, PA

Turkey with Maple Glaze
(page 31), Holiday Yams
(page 37), Homestyle Green
Beans (page 34) and
Cornbread Dressing
(page 33)

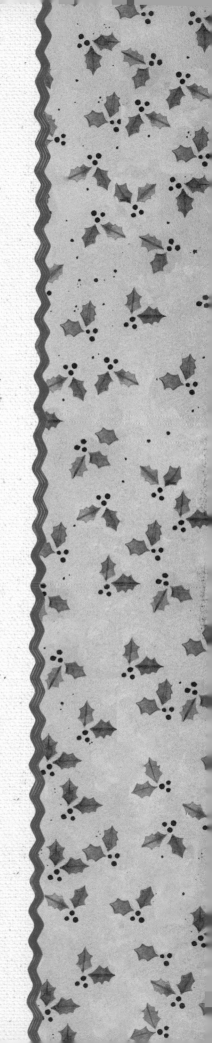

Christmas classics

Memories of foods like your grandmother's dressing or your aunt's light-as-a-feather yeast rolls always top the list of holiday gatherings of yesteryear. Here you'll find a treasure of equally enticing entrées, veggies, dressings…and of course desserts…that will reward you with rave reviews for years to come.

Best-Ever Baked Ham

Best-Ever Baked Ham

8- to 10-lb. smoked fully cooked ham
half (shank end)
8-oz. jar Dijon mustard

1-lb. pkg. brown sugar
12-oz. can cola-flavored beverage

Remove and discard skin from ham. Score fat on ham in a diamond design; place ham, fat side up, in a 13"x9" baking dish. Coat ham with mustard; pat with brown sugar. Pour cola into dish. Bake, uncovered, at 325 degrees for 2½ to 3 hours or until a meat thermometer inserted into center of ham, making sure it does not touch fat or bone, registers 140 degrees. (Do not baste.) Remove ham from dish, reserving drippings. Let ham stand.

Meanwhile, bring drippings to a boil in a 1½-quart saucepan over medium-high heat. Reduce heat to medium and simmer, uncovered, 20 minutes or until sauce thickens. Serve sauce with ham. Serves 16 to 18.

Turkey with Maple Glaze

(pictured on page 28)

12-lb. fresh turkey
1 c. butter, melted
1½ T. salt

2 t. pepper
⅔ c. pure maple syrup

Remove giblets and neck from turkey; reserve for other uses. Rinse turkey with cold water; pat dry. Place in a large roaster, breast-side down, in 2 inches of water. Bake, uncovered, at 350 degrees for one hour.

Turn turkey breast-side up; pour butter over turkey and sprinkle with salt and pepper. Bake, uncovered, 30 minutes; pour maple syrup over turkey and bake 30 more minutes or until a meat thermometer inserted into meaty part of thigh registers 167 degrees or to desired degree of doneness. Transfer turkey to a platter and let stand 30 to 45 minutes before slicing. Serves 10 to 12.

Juicy Prime Rib

¼ c. black pepper
2 T. ground white pepper
2 T. salt
1½ t. dried thyme

1½ t. garlic powder
1 t. onion powder
8- to 10-lb. boneless beef rib-eye roast

Combine first 6 ingredients; rub evenly over surface of roast. Place roast in a shallow roasting pan; insert a meat thermometer into thickest part of roast, making sure it does not touch fat or bone. Bake, uncovered, at 350 degrees for 13 minutes per pound or until thermometer registers 145 degrees (for medium-rare) or 160 degrees (medium). Cover with foil and let stand 15 minutes before carving. Serves 16 to 20.

Cumin Pork Roast with Wild Mushroom Sauce

3½-lb. boneless center-cut pork loin roast
1 T. ground cumin
1½ t. salt, divided
1¼ t. pepper, divided
2 T. butter or margarine
8-oz. pkg. sliced fresh mushrooms
¼ lb. sliced fresh oyster mushrooms
¼ lb. sliced fresh shiitake mushrooms
½ c. chopped shallots

1 clove garlic, minced
1 T. seeded and minced jalapeño pepper, divided
2 T. chopped fresh cilantro
2 T. chopped fresh oregano
1 t. ground cumin
2 T. all-purpose flour
¼ c. dry sherry
14½-oz. can chicken broth
1 T. butter or margarine

Place roast, fat side up, on a rack in a shallow roasting pan. Cut small slits in roast at ½-inch intervals. Combine one tablespoon cumin, one teaspoon salt and one teaspoon pepper; gently rub seasoning mixture over entire surface of roast.

Bake, uncovered, at 375 degrees for 50 minutes or until a meat thermometer inserted into thickest part registers 160 degrees. Let stand 10 to 15 minutes before slicing. Reserve drippings.

Meanwhile, melt 2 tablespoons butter in a large skillet over medium heat. Add mushrooms, shallots, garlic and one teaspoon jalapeño pepper; sauté 15 minutes or until mushrooms are very tender and beginning to brown. Remove from heat. Stir chopped cilantro, oregano, one teaspoon ground cumin, remaining ½ teaspoon salt and remaining ¼ teaspoon pepper into mushroom mixture; set aside.

Combine flour and sherry in a small bowl, whisking until smooth. Pour reserved drippings into a large skillet. Add chicken broth; bring to a boil and reduce heat to medium. Gradually whisk flour mixture into broth mixture; cook over medium heat until thickened, stirring constantly. Add one tablespoon butter and remaining 2 teaspoons jalapeño pepper; cook, stirring constantly, one minute. Stir in reserved mushroom mixture and cook 5 more minutes, stirring occasionally. Serve roast with sauce. Serves 6.

Memories of the Season

EVERY YEAR DURING THE LAST FEW DAYS BEFORE CHRISTMAS, we make a new "Memory List." The list has questions that stay the same, but with 4 children, our answers differ each year. We also add a new question every year. As we write our new list, we review the old year's answers. We laugh and laugh and it's a highlight of mine that I wait for each year.

Tammy Young
St. Peters, MO

Grilled Beef Tenderloin Diablo

1½ c. dry sherry
⅔ c. dark sesame oil
½ c. orange juice
1 small onion, minced
3 cloves garlic, pressed
2 bay leaves
2 T. chopped green onions
1 T. chopped fresh basil
1 T. chopped fresh chives

1 T. chopped fresh oregano
1 T. Worcestershire sauce
1 T. soy sauce
1 t. salt
1 t. pepper
1½ t. hot sauce
4- to 5-lb. beef tenderloin, trimmed
1 c. kosher salt

Combine first 15 ingredients in a large plastic freezer zipping bag. Add tenderloin; seal and chill 8 hours, turning occasionally. Remove tenderloin from marinade, discarding marinade. Roll tenderloin in kosher salt until meat is coated.

Grill, covered with grill lid, over medium-high heat (350 degrees to 400 degrees) about 30 to 40 minutes or until a meat thermometer inserted into thickest part of tenderloin registers 145 degrees (medium-rare) or 160 degrees (medium). Serves 8 to 10.

Cornbread Dressing

(pictured on page 28)

2 c. cornmeal
½ c. all-purpose flour
2 t. baking powder
1 t. baking soda
1 t. salt
1 t. sugar (optional)
6 eggs

2 c. buttermilk
2 T. bacon drippings or melted butter
½ c. butter or margarine
3 bunches green onions, chopped
4 celery ribs, chopped
16-oz. pkg. herb-seasoned stuffing mix
5 (14½-oz.) cans chicken broth

Combine first 5 ingredients, and, if desired, sugar in a large bowl. Stir together 2 eggs and buttermilk; add egg mixture to dry ingredients, stirring just until moistened.

Heat bacon drippings in a 10" cast-iron skillet or 9" round cake pan in a 425 degree oven 5 minutes. Stir hot drippings into batter. Pour batter into hot skillet.

Bake, uncovered, at 425 degrees for 25 minutes or until golden; cool and crumble.

Melt butter in a large skillet over medium heat; add green onions and celery and sauté until tender.

Stir together remaining 4 eggs in a large bowl; stir in cornbread, onion mixture, stuffing mix and broth until blended. Spoon dressing into one lightly greased 13"x9" baking dish and one lightly greased 9" square baking dish.

Bake 13"x9" dish, uncovered, at 350 degrees for one hour or until lightly browned. Bake 9" square dish, uncovered, 50 minutes or until lightly browned. Serves 12.

This tenderloin grills up extra juicy with a marinade of sherry and fresh herbs and a coating of kosher salt that seals in the juices.

Cover and freeze the unbaked dressing up to 3 months, if desired; thaw in the refrigerator for 8 hours and bake as directed.

Make-Ahead Mashed Potatoes

5 lbs. potatoes, peeled, quartered and
boiled
3-oz. pkg. cream cheese, softened

2 c. sour cream
1 T. butter or margarine, softened
Salt, pepper and paprika to taste

Mash potatoes in a large bowl; blend in cream cheese, sour cream and butter. Add salt, pepper and paprika to taste. Spread in a greased 13"x9" baking dish; cover and chill overnight. Bake, covered, at 350 degrees for 30 minutes. Serves 8 to 10.

Broccoli with Orange Sauce

Broccoli gets dressed up for the holidays with a zesty fresh orange sauce.

1 lb. broccoli, cut into spears
2 T. butter or margarine
1 T. cornstarch
1 c. orange juice, divided
1 T. minced fresh parsley
1 T. lemon juice

1 T. orange zest
½ t. dried thyme
½ t. dry mustard
¼ t. pepper
Garnish: orange slices or orange zest

Steam broccoli just until tender. In a separate saucepan, melt butter. Add cornstarch and ½ cup orange juice, stirring until blended. Stir in remaining orange juice, parsley and next 5 ingredients. Cook over medium heat until mixture thickens; pour over broccoli. Garnish, if desired. Serves 4.

Homestyle Green Beans

(pictured on page 28)

1½ lbs. fresh green beans, trimmed
½ c. balsamic vinegar
½ c. dried tomatoes
2 T. minced shallot

2 T. butter or olive oil
2 T. brown sugar
¼ t. salt
⅛ t. pepper

Cook beans in boiling water to cover 10 minutes or until crisp-tender. Drain and set aside.

Bring vinegar to a boil in a saucepan; remove from heat. Add tomatoes; let stand 10 minutes. Drain tomatoes, reserving vinegar. Coarsely chop tomatoes.

Cook shallot in butter in a large skillet over medium heat, stirring constantly, until tender. Add reserved vinegar, tomato, brown sugar, salt and pepper. Cook over low heat until sugar melts, stirring occasionally.

Add beans to skillet and toss gently. Cook just until thoroughly heated. Spoon mixture into a serving bowl. Serves 6.

Apple & Sausage Stuffing

Apple & Sausage Stuffing

1 lb. sweet Italian sausage
1 T. vegetable oil
1 large onion, diced
2 celery ribs, chopped
1 apple, peeled, cored and diced

2½ c. water
½ cup butter or margarine, melted
1 lb. herb-seasoned stuffing mix
1 t. fennel seeds

"This is a favorite of ours that your family will love."

CAROL TOMASETTI-RECORDS
WINDHAM, CT

Remove and discard casings from sausage. Brown sausage in a large skillet over medium heat, stirring until sausage crumbles and is no longer pink; drain. Remove sausage to a large bowl. Heat one tablespoon oil in skillet. Sauté onion, celery and apple until tender; remove from heat. Combine water and melted butter in a large bowl. Combine stuffing mix with water and butter; toss lightly until moistened. (You can add more water if you prefer moister stuffing.) Add fennel seeds to stuffing mix and blend. Add stuffing and onion mixture to sausage; mix thoroughly. Place stuffing in a lightly greased 13"x9" pan and bake, uncovered, at 350 degrees for 30 minutes. Serves 8 to 10.

Macaroni au Gratin

Macaroni au Gratin

8-oz. pkg. elbow macaroni (about 1¾ c.)
¼ c. butter or margarine
¼ c. all-purpose flour
2 c. milk
½ (16-oz.) pkg. process American cheese, cubed
1 T. minced onion
½ t. salt
½ t. Worcestershire sauce
¼ t. pepper
¼ t. dry mustard
2 T. Italian-seasoned bread crumbs
Butter or margarine

Cook macaroni according to package directions; drain and set aside.

Meanwhile, melt ¼ cup butter in a large heavy saucepan over low heat; whisk in flour until smooth. Cook one minute, whisking constantly. Gradually whisk in milk. Cook over medium heat, whisking constantly, until mixture is thickened and bubbly. Reduce heat and add cheese, onion, salt, Worcestershire sauce, pepper and mustard; stir until cheese melts. Add macaroni, and mix well.

Divide mixture evenly into 6 (8-ounce) greased ramekins, or a greased 2-quart baking dish. Sprinkle with bread crumbs and dot lightly with additional butter. Bake, uncovered, at 375 degrees for 20 to 30 minutes. Serves 4 to 6.

Holiday Yams

(pictured on page 28)

29-oz. can sliced peaches
2 T. cornstarch
⅔ c. brown sugar, packed
16-oz. can cranberry sauce
1 t. ground cinnamon
¼ c. butter or margarine
2 (40-oz.) cans yams, drained

Drain peaches, reserving juice. Stir together cornstarch and ¼ cup reserved juice. Pour remaining juice in a saucepan; stir in brown sugar, cranberry sauce, cinnamon and butter. Cook over medium heat until butter is melted, stirring constantly. Add cornstarch mixture; cook until thickened. Add yams and cook 10 minutes. Stir in peaches; cook 5 more minutes. Serves 10 to 12.

"One of my favorite recipes for holiday cooking…I can't get away without making it!"

LEAH-ANNE SCHNAPP,
EFFORT, PA

REFRESH YOUR COLLECTION OF HOLIDAY SERVING CONTAINERS…swap them with friends! Invite everyone to bring two serving dishes, glasses or bowls to a mix-and-match party to trade. Everyone goes home with something new.

Lane Cake

1 c. butter or margarine, softened
2 c. sugar
3 c. sifted cake flour
1 T. plus 1 t. baking powder
¾ c. milk
½ t. vanilla extract
¼ t. almond extract
8 egg whites
Lane Cake Filling
Seven-Minute Frosting

Beat butter at medium speed with an electric mixer until creamy; gradually add sugar, beating well.

Combine flour and baking powder; add to butter mixture alternately with milk, beginning and ending with flour mixture. Beat at low speed after each addition until blended. Stir in flavorings.

Beat egg whites at high speed until stiff peaks form; fold into batter. Pour into 3 greased and floured 9" round cake pans.

Bake at 325 degrees for 18 minutes or until a wooden toothpick inserted in center comes out clean. Cool in pans on wire racks 10 minutes; remove from pans and cool completely on wire racks.

Spread Lane Cake Filling between layers and on top of cake. Spread Seven-Minute Frosting on sides of cake. Serves 12.

Lane Cake Filling

½ c. butter or margarine
8 egg yolks
1½ c. sugar
1 c. chopped pecans
1 c. chopped raisins
1 c. flaked coconut
½ c. chopped maraschino cherries
⅓ c. bourbon or sherry

Melt butter in a heavy saucepan over low heat. Add egg yolks and sugar; cook, stirring vigorously, until sugar dissolves and mixture thickens (18 to 20 minutes). Remove from heat; stir in pecans and remaining ingredients. Cool completely. Makes 3½ cups.

Seven-Minute Frosting

1½ c. sugar
⅓ c. warm water
2 egg whites
1 T. light corn syrup
1 t. vanilla extract

Combine first 4 ingredients in top of a large double boiler; beat at low speed with an electric mixer 30 seconds or until blended.

Place over boiling water; beat constantly at high speed 7 to 9 minutes or until stiff peaks form and temperature reaches 160 degrees. Remove from heat. Add vanilla; beat 2 minutes or until frosting is spreading consistency. Makes 4½ cups.

Chocolate Pecan Pie

Chocolate Pecan Pie

(pictured on cover)

½ (15-oz.) pkg. refrigerated piecrusts
4 eggs
1 c. light corn syrup
6 T. butter or margarine, melted
½ c. granulated sugar
¼ c. light brown sugar, packed

1 T. vanilla extract
1 c. coarsely chopped pecans
1 c. (6 oz.) semisweet chocolate chips
Hot fudge topping, warmed
Frozen whipped topping
Chopped chocolate

Pecan pie is elevated to decadent status with the addition of chocolate inside and outside this classic holiday pie.

Fit piecrust into a 9" deep dish pie plate according to package directions; fold edges under and crimp. Whisk together eggs and next 5 ingredients until mixture is smooth; stir in chopped pecans and chocolate chips. Pour into piecrust. Bake on lowest oven rack at 350 degrees for one hour or until set. Drizzle each serving with hot fudge topping, dollop with whipped topping and sprinkle with chopped chocolate. Serves 8.

Filet Mignon with Mushrooms (page 42) and Roasted Asparagus (page 46)

In a wink of an eye

As the big day draws nigh, you'll savor the

simplicity…and the flavor…of these speedy recipes.

Just take a look at 5-ingredient Mandarin Pork Chops, 20-minute

Stroganoff Skillet and microwave-easy Chocolate-Peanut Butter Fudge.

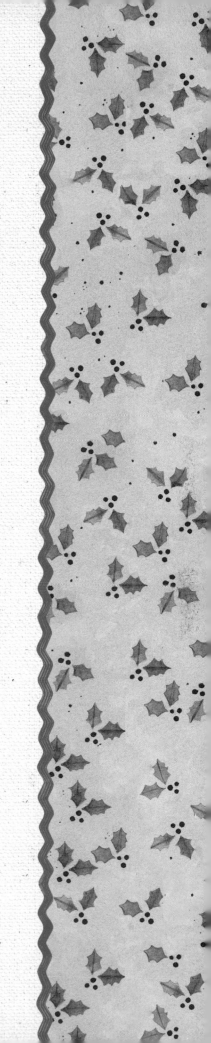

Filet Mignon with Mushrooms

(pictured on page 40)

4 (6-oz.) beef tenderloin filets
½ t. salt
½ t. pepper
½ t. garlic powder

12-oz. pkg. sliced mushrooms
4 cloves garlic, chopped
6 T. Marsala wine

Sprinkle each filet with salt, pepper and garlic powder; set aside.

Coat a large skillet with non-stick vegetable spray and heat to medium-high. Add mushrooms and garlic; cook for 5 minutes or until mushrooms are golden, stirring frequently. Remove from heat and set aside.

Arrange filets on a broiler pan about 4 inches from heat. Broil about 4 minutes on each side or to desired doneness.

Meanwhile, reheat mushroom mixture in skillet over medium-high heat. Add wine to mixture and bring to a boil; cook about 2 minutes or until wine is reduced. Place each steak on a serving plate and top with mushroom mixture. Serves 4.

"A terrific dinner party recipe…it's simple and quick but tastes like you spent hours on it."

SUSAN YOUNG
MADISON, AL

Mandarin Pork Chops

1 T. vegetable oil
4 to 6 (1"-thick) pork chops
11-oz. can mandarin oranges, drained

½ t. ground cloves
⅛ t. pepper

Heat oil in a large skillet over medium-high heat; add pork chops. Cook pork chops 3 to 5 minutes on each side. Top with oranges; sprinkle with cloves and pepper. Cover and cook over medium heat 15 minutes or until chops are done. Serves 4 to 6.

With a prep time of about 5 minutes, you can have this dish on the table in 25 minutes! While the chicken is baking, cook spaghetti noodles to go alongside.

Parmesan Baked Chicken

½ c. mayonnaise-type salad dressing
⅓ c. grated Parmesan cheese
¾ t. garlic powder

4 boneless, skinless chicken breasts
¾ c. Italian bread crumbs

Combine salad dressing, cheese and garlic powder in a medium bowl. Coat chicken with dressing mixture and top with bread crumbs. Arrange chicken on an ungreased baking sheet. Bake, uncovered, at 425 degrees for 15 to 20 minutes or until lightly golden and chicken is done. Serves 4.

Quick
Salisbury Steak

Quick Salisbury Steak

1 lb. ground beef
1½-oz. pkg. dry onion soup mix
2 eggs, beaten

2 (10¾-oz.) cans golden mushroom
soup

Combine ground beef, soup mix and eggs in a large bowl; form into 4 patties. Place patties in an ungreased 13"x9" baking dish; cover with soup. Bake, uncovered, at 350 degrees for 35 minutes. Serves 4.

Serve this family favorite over creamy mashed potatoes to soak in the savory mushroom sauce.

Jambalaya

Jambalaya

2 T. butter or margarine
7-oz. pkg. chicken-flavored
   rice vermicelli mix
2¾ c. water
¼ t. pepper
¼ t. hot pepper sauce

1 T. dried, minced onion
¼ c. diced celery
¼ c. diced green bell pepper
2 c. diced cooked ham
1 lb. cooked, peeled medium-size
   fresh shrimp

Melt butter in a large saucepan over medium heat. Add rice vermicelli mix and sauté just until golden. Stir in water and next 6 ingredients; reduce heat, cover and simmer 10 minutes. Add shrimp and cook for 5 minutes or until thoroughly heated. Serves 4 to 6.

Stroganoff Skillet

1 lb. ground round
1 onion, chopped
10¾-oz. can cream of mushroom soup
8-oz. container sour cream

1 c. beef broth
½ c. water
3 c. wide egg noodles, uncooked

Brown ground round and onion in a large skillet over medium heat; drain. Gradually add soup and remaining ingredients; bring to a boil. Cover, reduce heat and simmer 10 minutes or until noodles are tender. Serves 4 to 6.

BBQ Chicken Pizza

2 c. cooked and shredded boneless, skinless chicken breasts
½ to 1 c. barbecue sauce
1 prebaked pizza crust

1 red onion, sliced
1 green bell pepper, sliced
1 c. shredded mozzarella cheese

Combine chicken and barbecue sauce in a large bowl; spread over pizza crust. Arrange sliced onion and bell pepper over chicken; sprinkle with cheese. Bake at 450 degrees for 10 to 12 minutes or until cheese is melted. Serves 6 to 8.

Linguine with Tomato-Clam Sauce

2 T. butter or margarine
1 T. minced garlic
1 c. thinly sliced mushrooms
14½-oz. can chicken broth
2 (6½-oz.) cans chopped clams, drained and ¾ c. liquid reserved

14½-oz. can diced tomatoes, drained
1 t. dried parsley
Salt and pepper to taste
¼ c. white wine or chicken broth
8-oz. pkg. linguine, cooked

Melt butter in a saucepan over medium-high heat. Add garlic and sauté 30 seconds; add mushrooms and sauté one minute. Add broth, clams and reserved liquid and next 4 ingredients; bring to a boil and simmer 5 minutes. Serve sauce over cooked linguine. Serves 4 to 6.

For a thicker sauce, whisk together one tablespoon all-purpose flour with one tablespoon softened butter in a small bowl. Add to broth mixture, stirring until thickened.

It's best to use fresh asparagus for this recipe because neither frozen nor canned roast well.

Roasted Asparagus

(pictured on page 40)

1 lb. fresh asparagus
½ c. vertically sliced onion
½ c. sliced red bell pepper
1 T. olive oil

½ t. dried rosemary
⅛ t. garlic powder
½ T. balsamic vinegar

Place asparagus, onion and red bell pepper in a heavy roasting pan. Toss with oil, rosemary and garlic. Cook, uncovered, at 500 degrees for 10 minutes; drizzle with balsamic vinegar before serving. Serves 4.

Savory Limas

2 (9-oz.) pkgs. frozen baby lima beans
6 cloves garlic, chopped
2 T. butter or margarine

½ c. whipping cream
¼ t. salt

Place lima beans and garlic in boiling water to cover. Cook 10 to 12 minutes or until softened; drain. Stir in butter; mash with a potato masher. Add whipping cream and salt and mash until creamy. Serves 4.

"If you have a little extra time, use fresh corn on the cob. Just use the liquid from the corn instead of the milk called for in the recipe."

SHERRI SMITH
RAVENNA, OH

Creamed Corn

1 c. canned corn
½ t. milk
2 T. sugar
2 slices bacon, crisply cooked,
   crumbled and drippings reserved

3 T. all-purpose flour
½ c. water
Salt and pepper to taste

Combine corn and milk in a medium bowl; add sugar. Place corn mixture, bacon and bacon drippings in a large skillet.

Stir together flour and water in a measuring cup until smooth. Add enough additional water to the measuring cup to equal one cup. Add flour mixture to corn and cook over medium heat 10 to 15 minutes or until mixture is thickened; stir in salt and pepper to taste. Serves 4 to 6.

Chunky Applesauce

2 small cooking apples, cored, peeled
   and cubed
½ c. sugar

½ t. ground cinnamon
¼ c. water

Combine first 3 ingredients in a medium-size microwave-safe bowl; add water, stirring gently. Cover and microwave on HIGH (100%) for 7 minutes; stir well. Makes 2 cups.

Roasted Walnut & Pear Salad

Roasted Walnut & Pear Salad

1 c. walnuts
2 T. butter or margarine, melted
¼ c. brown sugar, packed
1 head romaine lettuce, torn
2 c. thinly sliced pears

2 c. halved grape tomatoes
4-oz. pkg. crumbled blue cheese
8-oz. bottle raspberry white wine
    vinegar salad dressing

Toast walnuts in a medium skillet in butter until golden; add brown sugar and stir over low heat until walnuts are hardened with glaze.

Place lettuce in a large serving bowl; layer with pears and tomatoes. Add walnuts to salad; sprinkle with blue cheese and toss with vinegar dressing. Serves 6 to 8.

"This is a wonderful choice for a formal dinner or a casual, warm family gathering. Use fresh pears for the best flavor."

LAURIE JOHNSON
ROSENBERG, TX

Yummy Garden Bread

2 (12-oz.) tubes refrigerated biscuits
5 slices bacon, crisply cooked and
    crumbled
¼ c. chopped green bell pepper

¼ c. chopped onion
½ c. shredded sharp Cheddar cheese
¼ c. butter or margarine, melted

Quarter biscuits and place in a large bowl. Add bacon and remaining ingredients; toss with biscuits to coat. Spoon into a lightly greased 12-cup Bundt pan; bake at 350 degrees for 35 minutes or until lightly browned. Immediately invert onto a platter and serve hot. Serves 8.

"This is a savory version of the popular Monkey Bread."

CARA KILLINGSWORTH
SHAMROCK, TX

Chocolate Chip
Pudding Cake

Chocolate Chip Pudding Cake

3.4-oz. pkg. non-instant chocolate
  pudding mix
2 c. milk

18¼-oz. pkg. chocolate cake mix
12-oz. pkg. semi-sweet chocolate chips
Vanilla ice cream

Bring pudding and milk to a boil in a 2-quart saucepan over medium heat, stirring constantly. Remove from heat and stir in cake mix just until blended. Spread mixture into a greased and floured 13"x9" baking dish. Sprinkle evenly with chocolate chips. Bake at 325 degrees for 35 minutes. Serve warm with ice cream. Serves 15.

Mom's No-Bake Cookies

1 c. sugar
2 T. baking cocoa
¼ c. butter or margarine
¼ c. milk

¼ t. vanilla extract
¼ c. creamy peanut butter
1½ c. quick-cooking oats, uncooked
¼ c. toasted wheat germ

Combine sugar, cocoa, butter and milk in a large saucepan; cook, stirring constantly, over medium heat until sugar is melted. Remove from heat and add vanilla and peanut butter; stir until peanut butter is melted. Add oats and wheat germ to pan; stir until oats are well coated. Drop by tablespoonfuls onto wax paper-lined baking sheets and cool in refrigerator. Makes 2 dozen cookies.

Easiest Pecan Pralines

1 lb. box brown sugar
1 c. whipping cream

2 c. pecan halves
2 T. butter

Stir together brown sugar and whipping cream in a 4-quart microwave-safe bowl. Microwave on HIGH (100%) for 5 minutes; stir well. Microwave 4 more minutes; stir well. Microwave one more minute. Remove mixture from microwave; stir in pecan halves and butter. Stir one minute or just until candy starts to lose its luster. Working rapidly, drop by rounded teaspoonfuls onto wax paper; let stand until firm. Makes about 3 dozen.

Microwave pralines . . . what could be easier? Drop the candy onto wax paper quickly before it hardens...a second pair of hands is helpful.

Chocolate-Peanut Nuggets

1 T. oil
3 T. baking cocoa
24 oz. white almond bark

12-oz. pkg. semi-sweet chocolate chips
16 oz. unsalted, dry roasted peanuts
16 oz. salted, dry roasted peanuts

Place oil, cocoa, white almond bark and chocolate chips in a *3-quart slow cooker*. Cover and cook on LOW setting 2 hours or until chocolate is melted and smooth. Add peanuts; stir well. Drop by tablespoonfuls onto wax paper; cool. Makes about 8 dozen candies.

Chocolate-Peanut Butter Fudge

1 c. creamy peanut butter
1 c. butter
1-lb. pkg. powdered sugar

⅛ t. salt
¼ c. baking cocoa
1 t. vanilla extract

Combine peanut butter and butter in a large microwave-safe bowl. Microwave on HIGH (100%) for 2 minutes; stir. Microwave on HIGH 2 more minutes. Add powdered sugar and remaining ingredients; stir until smooth.

Line a 13"x9" pan with plastic wrap; press fudge into pan, smooth top and refrigerate until firm. Cut into bite-size pieces. Makes about 2½ pounds.

No candy thermometer is needed here, making this quick fudge extra easy!

Chocolate Ice Box Pie

5-oz. bar chocolate candy
12-oz. container frozen whipped
    topping, thawed

6-oz. chocolate pie crust

Place candy in a small microwave-safe bowl. Microwave on HIGH (100%) for 2 minutes or until melted, stirring once. Fold in whipped topping. Spoon chocolate mixture into pie crust; chill 3 hours or until firm enough to slice. Serves 6 to 8.

Next-Day Chicken Bake
(page 53)

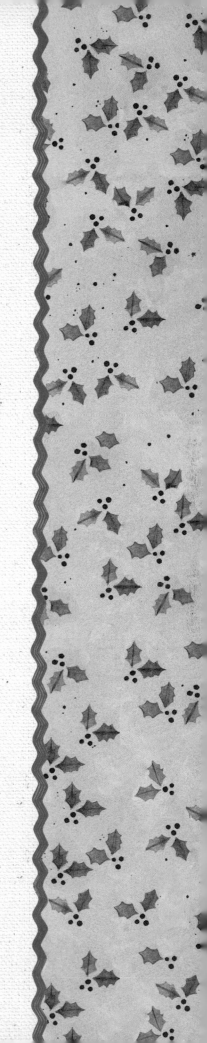

Make-Ahead favorites

Stock up your refrigerator or freezer a day ahead or even a

week or month ahead. So after a day of Christmas shopping,

dinner will be a breeze! Recipes, such as Overnight Asian Salad,

Next-Day Chicken Bake, Slow-Cooker Fajitas and Date-Nut Dessert

Cheese, that you can make and chill for four days help keep

your days simple and your dinners delish!

Overnight Asian Salad

Cheese Logs

8-oz. pkg. cream cheese, softened
2 c. shredded Cheddar cheese
2 c. shredded Swiss cheese
1 t. mustard

1 t. Worcestershire sauce
1 t. paprika
1 t. lemon juice
2 c. chopped nuts

Combine all ingredients except the nuts; mix well. Divide mixture in half; shape each half into a log. Roll logs in chopped nuts; wrap in plastic wrap and chill until ready to serve. Serve with assorted crackers. Serves 20.

"These Cheese Logs freeze well. They're perfect to have around for drop-in guests during the holidays!"

SALLY ANDERSON
SPRINGFIELD, MN

Overnight Asian Salad

¾ c. vegetable oil
½ c. sugar
½ c. white vinegar
2 pkgs. Oriental ramen noodles with seasoning packets

1 head cabbage, shredded
1 bunch green onions, chopped
1 c. sliced almonds, toasted
1 c. roasted sunflower seeds

Whisk together oil, sugar, vinegar and seasoning packets from noodles; chill dressing overnight. Crush noodles in a serving bowl; add cabbage, onions, almonds and sunflower seeds. Pour oil mixture over salad; toss gently. Serves 10 to 12.

Go ahead and shred the cabbage, chop the green onions and toast the almonds the night before, too. Then everything will be ready when you are!

Next-Day Chicken Bake

(pictured on page 50)

1 c. diced cooked chicken
1 c. prepared rice
¼ c. chopped almonds, toasted
1 green onion, chopped
10¾-oz. can cream of mushroom soup
½ t. salt

1 to 2 t. lemon juice
½ c. mayonnaise
¾ c. chopped celery
2 to 3 eggs, hard-boiled, peeled and chopped
1 c. crushed potato chips

Combine all ingredients except potato chips in a 2-quart casserole dish; cover and chill overnight. Sprinkle with potato chips. Bake, uncovered, at 375 degrees for 30 minutes. Serves 4.

"Fruit salad and freshly baked muffins make quick accompaniments with this classic chicken casserole."

LUCILLE DAHLBERG
GLENDALE, CA

Harvest Beans

16-oz. can kidney beans, drained and rinsed
15½-oz. can butter beans, drained
15-oz. can pork and beans
½ c. catsup
1 t. prepared mustard

½ c. brown sugar, packed
1 medium onion, chopped
½ lb. ground chuck, browned
½ lb. bacon, crisply cooked and crumbled

Stir together all ingredients in a *4-quart slow cooker*. Cover and cook on HIGH setting 2 hours or until thoroughly heated. Serves 4 to 6.

Frank's Chicken

4 potatoes, peeled and quartered
1 carrot, chopped
1 onion, diced
1 celery rib, chopped
1 t. salt, divided
4 chicken legs
4 chicken thighs

½ c. chicken broth
¼ c. white wine
½ T. paprika
2 t. garlic powder
½ t. dried rosemary
½ t. dried basil
2 T. cornstarch (optional)

Place first 4 ingredients in a *4-quart slow cooker*; sprinkle with ½ teaspoon salt. Arrange chicken on top. Pour broth and wine over chicken; sprinkle with remaining ½ teaspoon salt, paprika and next 3 ingredients.

Cover and cook on HIGH setting one hour. Reduce heat to LOW setting and cook 6 hours. Remove chicken and vegetables to a serving platter. Stir cornstarch into juices in slow cooker, if desired, and cook on HIGH setting until thickened. Serve gravy over chicken. Serves 4.

INVITE FRIENDS TO A SOUPER SUPPER POTLUCK. Line up slow cookers filled with hearty soups, plus one for hot cider and one for fruit cobbler. Complete the menu with a basketful of bread.

French Dip au Jus

2 c. beef broth
2/3 c. brown sugar, packed
1/4 t. seasoned salt
1 t. liquid smoke

1/3 c. soy sauce
3 to 4 lb. sirloin tip roast, cut in half
12 hoagie buns
12 slices Swiss cheese

Combine first 5 ingredients in a *5-quart slow cooker*; add meat. Cover and cook on HIGH setting one hour. Reduce heat to LOW setting and cook 8 hours.

Remove meat from slow cooker, reserving broth; shred meat with 2 forks and one cup reserved broth. Place meat evenly on buns and top each with a cheese slice. Serve remaining broth for dipping. Serves 12.

Slow-Cooker Fajitas

1 1/2 lbs. beef round steak (1/2" thick)
14.5-oz. can diced tomatoes, drained
1 onion, sliced
1 green bell pepper, cut into strips
1 red bell pepper, cut into strips
1 jalapeño, chopped
1 T. chopped fresh cilantro
2 cloves garlic, minced

1 t. chili powder
1 t. ground cumin
1 t. ground coriander
1/4 t. salt
8 to 10 (8") flour tortillas
Garnishes: sour cream, guacamole, salsa, shredded lettuce, shredded cheese

Place steak in a *4- to 5-quart slow cooker*. Combine vegetables and seasonings; spoon over steak. Cover and cook on HIGH setting 4 hours. Shred meat using 2 forks. With a slotted spoon, spoon meat mixture over tortillas and garnish with favorite toppings. Serves 8 to 10.

BBQ Ribs

1 t. salt
1/2 t. pepper
3 to 4 lbs. baby back pork ribs, racks cut in half

1 onion, sliced
18-oz. bottle barbecue sauce

Sprinkle salt and pepper evenly over ribs; let stand 5 minutes.

Place onion slices in a lightly greased *7-quart slow cooker*. Add ribs and pour sauce over ingredients in slow cooker. Cover and cook on HIGH setting 5 hours. Remove ribs; cover to keep warm.

Pour drippings and sauce from slow cooker into a bowl. Place ice cubes over surface of sauce to cover. Place sauce in the refrigerator for 30 minutes. Remove from refrigerator; discard ice cubes and solidified fat. Heat remaining sauce to serve. Serves 6 to 8.

Lasagna Rolls

Lasagna Rolls

11 lasagna noodles, uncooked
1 lb. ground beef
1 c. chopped onion
1 clove garlic, minced
26-oz. jar commercial spaghetti sauce
   with mushrooms and ripe olives
¼ c. dry white wine
3 T. chopped fresh parsley
½ t. salt

3 c. ricotta cheese
1 c. (4 oz.) shredded mozzarella
   cheese
2 eggs, lightly beaten
2 T. grated Parmesan cheese
⅓ c. fine, dry bread crumbs
1 t. dried Italian seasoning
½ c. grated Parmesan cheese

Cook lasagna noodles according to package directions; drain. Cut in half crosswise and set aside.

Cook beef, onion and garlic in a large skillet until beef is crumbled and no longer pink; drain. Add spaghetti sauce, wine, parsley and salt, stirring well. Cover and simmer 10 minutes, stirring occasionally. Remove from heat and set aside.

Combine ricotta cheese and next 5 ingredients, stirring well. Spread ricotta mixture evenly over lasagna noodles. Roll up jelly roll fashion, starting at narrow end. Place lasagna rolls, seam side down, in a lightly greased 13"x9" baking dish. Pour meat sauce over rolls and sprinkle with ½ cup Parmesan cheese.

Freeze tightly covered casserole up to one month. To serve, thaw in refrigerator. Bake, covered, at 375 degrees for 30 minutes. Uncover and bake 15 more minutes or until thoroughly heated. Serves 8 to 10.

Double this casserole when you make it to have one to keep and one to either give away or freeze for holiday company.

The Best Pot Roast Ever

4 lb. sirloin tip roast, cut in half
1 T. vegetable oil
1-oz. pkg. Ranch salad dressing mix
.7-oz. pkg. Italian salad dressing mix
4 potatoes, peeled and cubed (about
   2½ lbs.)

8 carrots, thickly sliced
1½ c. water
.87-oz. pkg. brown gravy mix
1 t. salt
½ t. pepper

Brown roast in a large skillet in hot oil over medium heat 12 minutes or until browned on all sides.

Place roast in a *6-quart slow cooker.* Sprinkle Ranch dressing mix and Italian dressing mix over roast. Place potatoes and carrots over roast. Combine water, brown gravy mix, salt and pepper; pour over vegetables and meat. Cover and cook on LOW setting 8 hours. Serves 6 to 8.

Slow cookers don't brown food, so sear meat or poultry in a skillet for extra flavor and added eye appeal…searing also cooks off excess fat.

Serve this whenever you want to serve a not-too-sweet dessert.

Date-Nut Dessert Cheese

⅔ c. walnuts, lightly toasted
⅔ c. chopped dates
8 oz. sharp Cheddar cheese, cut into 1" pieces

8-oz. pkg. cream cheese, softened and cut into 1" pieces
3 to 4 T. dark rum

Process walnuts in a food processor until coarsely chopped. Remove walnuts and set aside.

Add dates and process one minute or until finely chopped. Add Cheddar cheese, cream cheese and rum. Process 2 minutes, scraping sides of bowl occasionally.

Line a 2-cup mold with plastic wrap, extending plastic wrap over edges of mold. Spoon cheese mixture into mold, pressing firmly with the back of a spoon. Bring ends of plastic wrap over cheese mixture.

Cover and chill at least 4 hours and up to 4 days. To serve, unmold cheese and remove plastic wrap. Press reserved walnuts on top and sides of cheese. Serve with gingersnaps and apple and pear slices. Makes 2 cups.

Cookies & Cream Dessert

1 lb., 2-oz. pkg. chocolate sandwich cookies, crushed
½ c. butter or margarine, melted
8-oz. pkg. cream cheese, softened
2 (3.4-oz.) pkgs. vanilla instant pudding mix

3 c. milk
8-oz. container frozen whipped topping, thawed

Mix cookie crumbs with butter; reserve one cup of mixture. Press remaining mixture in the bottom of a 13"x9" dish; set aside.

Beat cream cheese at medium speed with an electric mixer. Add pudding mix and milk; beat until smooth. Fold in whipped topping. Spread over cookie mixture and sprinkle with reserved cookie mixture; chill one hour. Serves 15.

Turn store-bought cookies into ice cream sandwiches!

Spread softened ice cream on one cookie and top with another cookie. Roll edges of ice cream in coarsely chopped red & white peppermint candies and freeze until solid.

Cookies & Cream Dessert

Turkey-Cheddar-
Broccoli Strata
(page 63)

Second Time around

You can reinvent holiday leftovers into scrumptious meals for the rest of the year with these clever recipes. Slice the leftover bird to roll Cranberry-Turkey Wraps, chop the rest of the ham for Ham-Stuffed Baked Potatoes, or use extras from both entrées to stir up creamy Use-Your-Noodle Casserole.

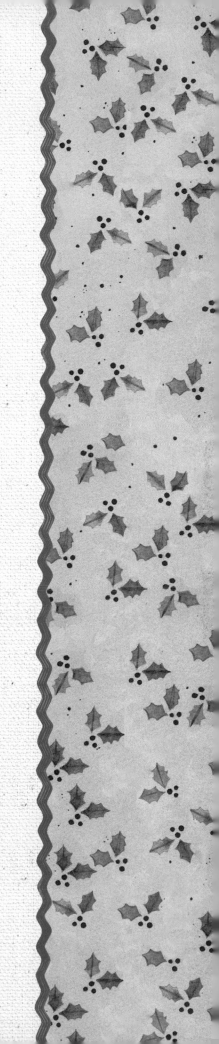

Turkey-Walnut
Salad

Italian Bread Salad

4 c. cubed Italian bread, toasted
3 tomatoes, diced and juice reserved
1 red onion, diced

1¾ c. chopped fresh basil leaves
1 c. olive oil
Salt and pepper to taste

Combine bread cubes, tomatoes and reserved juice, onion and basil in a large serving bowl. Add olive oil and toss to coat. Add salt and pepper to taste. Serves 10.

"This is a terrific way to use up leftover bread."

DAGMAR CIANELLI
DELAWARE, OH

Turkey–Walnut Salad

2 c. chopped cooked turkey
½ c. dried cranberries
½ c. light mayonnaise
¼ c. chopped walnuts, toasted
3 T. chopped fresh parsley
2 T. Dijon mustard

2 stalks celery, sliced
1 small red onion, chopped
 (about ½ c.)
¼ t. salt
¼ t. freshly ground pepper
Mixed salad greens

Stir together first 10 ingredients in a large bowl. Cover and chill at least 30 minutes. Serve over salad greens. Serves 10.

Turkey–Cheddar–Broccoli Strata

(pictured on page 60)

1 T. butter or margarine, softened
½ (12-oz.) pkg. French bread loaves,
 cubed
2 c. chopped cooked turkey
10-oz. pkg. frozen broccoli flowerets,
 thawed and chopped
½ c. diced celery
2 c. (8 oz.) shredded sharp Cheddar
 cheese

6 eggs, lightly beaten
2 c. milk
3 T. all-purpose flour
1 t. salt
1 t. curry powder
1 t. dry mustard
1 t. Worcestershire sauce
½ t. pepper

You can also make this in a 13"x9" baking dish…just adjust the baking time to 45 minutes.

Grease bottom and sides of 7 (10-ounce) custard cups with butter. Layer half each of bread cubes, turkey, broccoli, celery and Cheddar cheese in custard cups; repeat layers, ending with Cheddar cheese.

Whisk together eggs and next 7 ingredients in a large bowl; pour evenly over cheese, pressing down lightly to absorb liquid. Cover and chill 8 hours.

Bake, uncovered, at 350 degrees for 30 minutes or until golden. Let stand 10 minutes before serving. Serves 7.

Cranberry-Turkey Wraps

"Try dipping these wraps in extra cranberry sauce too!"

LYNN WILLIAMS
MUNCIE, IN

½ c. water
½ c. brown sugar, packed
⅓ c. granulated sugar
¼ c. cider vinegar
2 c. cranberries
½ c. raisins
½ c. chopped sweet onion
1 T. fresh ginger, peeled and finely chopped
½ t. red pepper flakes

2 (3-oz.) pkgs. cream cheese, softened
1½ c. shredded sharp white Cheddar cheese
1 t. curry powder
6 (10") flour tortillas
1½ lbs. cooked turkey slices
½ c. fresh cilantro, chopped and divided
6 T. chopped walnuts, divided

Add water, sugars and vinegar to a heavy saucepan; cook over medium heat until sugars dissolve, stirring often. Stir in cranberries, raisins, onion, ginger and red pepper; bring to a boil and cook 5 to 10 minutes until mixture thickens, stirring occasionally. Cool; cover and chill.

Combine cream cheese, Cheddar cheese and curry powder in a small bowl; stir well. Spread about 3 tablespoons cheese mixture over ⅔ of tortilla, leaving a one-inch border; top with several turkey slices. Spread 2 to 3 tablespoons cranberry mixture on top; sprinkle with one heaping teaspoon cilantro and one tablespoon walnuts. Roll up tortillas starting with filled side, folding sides in; wrap tightly in parchment paper or aluminum foil. Arrange wraps on a baking sheet; bake at 350 degrees for 5 to 10 minutes or just until warm. Slice wraps in half diagonally and arrange on a serving plate; serve warm. Serves 6.

Holiday Leftovers Casserole

You can use chicken instead of turkey in this recipe and enjoy it all year long. Substitute one jar of diced red bell peppers for the jar of pimientos, if desired.

7-oz. pkg. spaghetti, broken into 2" pieces
2 c. chopped cooked turkey
¾ c. diced ham
2-oz. jar diced pimento, drained
¼ c. minced green bell pepper

¼ small onion, grated
10¾-oz. can cream of mushroom soup
½ c. chicken or turkey broth
⅛ t. celery salt
⅛ t. pepper
1½ c. (6 oz.) shredded Cheddar cheese

Cook spaghetti according to package directions in a large Dutch oven; drain well and return spaghetti to pot.

Stir in turkey and next 8 ingredients; cook 7 minutes or until thoroughly heated. Remove from heat and stir in one cup cheese. Pour into a lightly greased 8" square baking dish. Sprinkle evenly with remaining ½ cup cheese. Bake, uncovered, at 350 degrees for 15 minutes or until cheese melts. Serves 4 to 6.

Cranberry-Turkey
Wraps

Easy Turkey Pot Pie

1½ c. frozen mixed corn, peas and
    carrots
1½ c. chopped cooked turkey
2 (10¾-oz.) cans cream of chicken soup

1 c. biscuit baking mix
¾ c. milk
1 egg

Stir together vegetables, turkey and soup; pour into an ungreased 9" pie pan. Combine baking mix, milk and egg in a medium bowl; pour over vegetable mixture and stir. Bake, uncovered, at 400 degrees for 35 minutes. Serves 8.

Fiesta Turkey Soup

1 medium onion, diced
1 t. vegetable oil
1 clove garlic, minced
3 c. chopped cooked turkey or chicken
15-oz. can chili beans
3½ c. chicken or turkey broth
11-oz. can whole kernel corn with red
    and green bell peppers, drained

10-oz. can diced tomatoes and green
    chilies
½ t. chili powder
½ t. ground cumin
⅛ t. salt
⅛ t. pepper
Toppings: sour cream, shredded
    Mexican four-cheese blend

Sauté onion in hot oil in a large Dutch oven over medium heat 7 minutes or until tender. Add garlic and sauté one minute. Stir in turkey and next 8 ingredients. Bring to a boil, stirring occasionally; reduce heat and simmer 15 minutes. Serve with desired toppings. Serves 8.

Use-Your-Noodle Casserole

2 T. butter or margarine
2 T. all-purpose flour
1 c. milk
½ c. cubed cooked ham
½ c. cubed cooked chicken
1 c. cooked wide egg noodles

¼ c. chopped celery
¼ t. salt
¼ t. pepper
¼ c. shredded Cheddar cheese
Paprika to taste (optional)

Melt butter in a large saucepan over low heat; stir in flour and heat until bubbly. Slowly add milk, stirring constantly, until mixture is thick and smooth. Remove from heat; stir in ham, chicken, noodles, celery, salt and pepper. Transfer to an ungreased 1½-quart casserole dish. Bake at 400 degrees for 15 minutes. Sprinkle with cheese and, if desired, paprika. Bake 5 to 10 more minutes or until cheese is bubbly. Serves 4.

Ham-Stuffed
Baked Potatoes

Ham-Stuffed Baked Potatoes

4 large potatoes (about 3 lbs.)	½ c. sour cream
1 T. butter or margarine	¼ t. salt
3 c. chopped cooked ham	¼ t. pepper
1 small onion, diced	¾ c. shredded Parmesan cheese
2 cloves garlic, minced	Garnish: chopped fresh chives

Bake potatoes at 450 degrees for one hour or until tender. Allow to cool to touch.

Cut potatoes in half lengthwise; scoop out pulp and place in a bowl, leaving shells intact. Set aside pulp and shells.

Melt butter in a small skillet over medium-high heat; add chopped ham, diced onion and minced garlic and sauté until onion is tender.

Mash potato pulp; stir in ham mixture, sour cream, salt and pepper. Stuff shells evenly with potato mixture; sprinkle evenly with Parmesan cheese. Place in a 13"x9" baking dish or pan. Bake, uncovered, at 350 degrees for 25 to 30 minutes. Garnish, if desired. Serves 8.

Leftover Potato Pancakes

16-oz. pkg. frozen whole kernel corn, thawed
1 small onion, finely chopped
½ c. chopped green onions
2 t. vegetable oil
2 c. mashed potatoes

½ c. all-purpose flour
2 eggs, lightly beaten
¾ t. salt
½ t. freshly ground pepper
Salsa

Cook first 3 ingredients in hot oil in a large non-stick skillet over medium-high heat, stirring constantly, until crisp-tender. Remove from heat.

Combine mashed potatoes, flour and eggs, stirring well; stir in corn mixture, salt and pepper.

Lightly grease a large skillet. Place skillet over medium heat until hot. Drop mixture by rounded tablespoonfuls into skillet; cook 3 minutes on each side or until golden, wiping skillet with a paper towel as necessary. Drain; serve with salsa. Makes 14 pancakes.

Spiced Eggnog Pound Cake

1 c. butter, softened
3 c. granulated sugar
6 eggs
3 c. sifted cake flour
¾ t. baking powder
½ t. salt
1 c. refrigerated or canned eggnog
2 t. vanilla extract

2 T. brandy (optional)
1 t. ground cinnamon
¾ t. freshly grated nutmeg
½ t. ground allspice
¼ t. ground cloves
Powdered sugar
1 c. sifted powdered sugar
2 T. plus 1 t. whipping cream

Generously grease and flour a 12-cup Bundt pan; set aside.

Beat butter at medium speed with an electric mixer about 2 minutes or until creamy. Gradually add granulated sugar, beating 5 to 7 minutes. Add eggs, one at a time, beating just until yellow disappears.

Combine flour, baking powder and salt. Add to butter mixture alternately with one cup eggnog, beginning and ending with flour mixture. Beat at low speed just until blended after each addition. Stir in vanilla and, if desired, brandy.

Pour half of batter into prepared pan. Stir cinnamon and next 3 ingredients into remaining batter. Spoon spice batter over plain batter. Swirl batters together, using a knife.

Bake at 350 degrees for 50 to 55 minutes or until a long toothpick inserted in center comes out clean. Cool in pan on a wire rack 15 minutes. Remove cake from pan; cool on wire rack. Place cake on a cake plate; dust with powdered sugar.

Combine one cup powdered sugar and whipping cream, stirring until smooth. Drizzle glaze over cake. Serves 16.

Eggnog Fudge

Eggnog Fudge

2 c. sugar
1 c. refrigerated eggnog
2 T. butter
2 T. light corn syrup
¼ c. chopped pecans, toasted

¼ c. slivered almonds, toasted and chopped
½ c. chopped red candied cherries
1 t. vanilla extract

Candied cherries and toasted nuts flavor this creamy fudge that's made with leftover eggnog.

Line an 8"x4" loaf pan with aluminum foil; butter foil and set aside.

Combine first 4 ingredients in a 4-quart heavy saucepan. Cook over medium heat, stirring constantly, until mixture comes to a boil. Wash down crystals from sides of pan, using a pastry brush dipped in hot water. Insert a candy thermometer into eggnog mixture. Cook, stirring occasionally, until thermometer registers 238 degrees. Remove pan from heat and cool sugar mixture, undisturbed, until temperature drops to 190 degrees (15 to 18 minutes).

Stir in pecans and remaining 3 ingredients; beat with a wooden spoon until fudge thickens and just begins to lose its gloss (5 to 8 minutes). Pour candy into prepared pan. Cool completely; cut into squares. Makes about 1½ pounds.

Weekend Beef Burgundy
(page 77)

Potluck
pleasers

Hosting a potluck where everyone brings a favorite dish makes

holiday get-togethers oh-so memorable! Whether you're the host or

you're simply attending, mouthwatering casseroles like Hot Chicken

Salad, Cajun Seafood Fettuccine and Ziti with Spinach & Cheese

will have everyone wanting the recipes!

Mom's Broccoli
Casserole

Mom's Broccoli Casserole

2 (12-oz.) pkgs. fresh broccoli flowerets
2 c. fresh cauliflower flowerets
1 c. sliced carrots
½ c. butter or margarine, melted
10¾-oz. can cream of mushroom soup

1 c. mayonnaise
1 c. shredded sharp Cheddar cheese
½ c. chopped onion
1 c. crushed round buttery crackers
 (about 18 crackers)

Bring a large pot of water to a boil; add broccoli, cauliflower and carrots. Boil 3 to 4 minutes or until vegetables are crisp-tender. Drain and set aside.

Pour melted butter into a 13"x9" baking dish; add cooked vegetables and set aside. Mix together soup, mayonnaise, cheese and onion in a medium bowl. Spread mixture over vegetables; top with crushed crackers. Bake, uncovered, at 350 degrees for 30 minutes. Serves 8.

Old-Fashioned Potato Casserole

28-oz. pkg. frozen hashbrowns with
 onions and peppers
2 (10¾-oz.) cans cream of chicken soup
16-oz. container sour cream

2 c. shredded Cheddar cheese
2 c. crushed corn flake cereal
½ c. butter or margarine, melted

Spread hashbrowns in a lightly greased 13"x9" baking dish. Stir together soup and sour cream; spread on top of hashbrowns. Sprinkle with cheese; top with crushed corn flakes and drizzle with butter. Bake, uncovered, at 350 degrees for 30 to 35 minutes. Serves 6 to 8.

Hot Chicken Salad

¼ c. butter or margarine
½ c. chopped onion
4-oz. jar pimentos
6-oz. pkg. slivered almonds
⅓ green bell pepper, diced
4-oz. can mushroom pieces, drained

1 c. chopped celery
4 c. diced cooked chicken
1 c. mayonnaise
10¾-oz. can cream of celery soup
1 t. salt
1 c. crushed corn flake cereal

Melt butter in a large skillet over medium-high heat. Add onion and next 5 ingredients; sauté until vegetables are tender. Place in an ungreased 13"x9" baking dish. Add chicken, mayonnaise, soup and salt; stir well. Sprinkle with crushed corn flakes; bake, uncovered, at 350 degrees for 30 minutes. Serves 8.

Shoepeg & Green Bean Casserole

2 (7-oz.) cans shoepeg corn, drained
14½-oz. can green beans, drained
10¾-oz. can cream of celery soup
1 c. sour cream

1 c. shredded Cheddar cheese
1 c. crushed round buttery crackers
  (about 18 crackers)
¼ c. butter or margarine, melted

Stir together corn, beans, soup, sour cream and cheese; spread in a greased 2-quart baking dish. Top with cracker crumbs; drizzle with melted butter. Bake, uncovered, at 350 degrees for one hour or until golden. Serves 6 to 8.

"Sometimes this casserole serves only 4 in my family!"

SHELIA COLLIER
KINGWOOD, TN

Cajun Seafood Fettuccine

¾ c. butter or margarine
2 (10-oz) pkgs. frozen seasoned
  vegetable blend
1 T. Cajun seasoning
½ t. garlic powder
¼ c. all-purpose flour
¼ c. water
16-oz. pkg. processed cheese, cubed

2 c. half-and-half
1½ lbs. medium-size fresh shrimp,
  peeled and deveined
1½ lbs. lump crabmeat, shell pieces
  removed
12-oz. pkg. fettuccine, cooked
1 c. shredded colby-Jack cheese

Melt butter in a large Dutch oven; add vegetables and sauté 5 minutes or until tender. Sprinkle with Cajun seasoning and garlic powder; set aside.

Combine flour and water; stir well. Add flour mixture to Dutch oven; stir well. Stir in cubed cheese and half-and-half; continue stirring until cheese is melted. Add shrimp and crabmeat to vegetable mixture; let simmer on medium-low heat for 5 minutes. Stir in fettuccine; pour into an ungreased 13"x9" baking dish. Sprinkle with colby-Jack cheese. Bake, uncovered, at 350 degrees for 20 minutes. Let stand 15 minutes before serving. Serves 8.

Create a family cookbook! At your next family potluck, have everyone share their favorite recipes and any memories or even photos that go with the recipes. The copy shop can easily make copies and bind them...everyone will want one!

Shoepeg & Green Bean
Casserole

*"Three types of cheese
are added to this ziti
casserole!"*

KAREN PILCHER
BURLESON, TX

Ziti with Spinach & Cheese

2 (10-oz.) pkgs. frozen chopped
  spinach, cooked and drained
15-oz. container ricotta cheese
3 eggs, beaten
⅔ c. grated Parmesan cheese
¼ t. salt

¼ t. pepper
16-oz. pkg. ziti pasta, cooked
26-oz. jar spaghetti sauce
2 t. dried oregano
16-oz. pkg. shredded mozzarella
  cheese

Combine spinach, ricotta cheese, eggs, Parmesan cheese, salt and pepper; set aside.
Combine pasta, spaghetti sauce and oregano; place half the pasta mixture in an
ungreased 13"x9" baking dish. Layer with spinach mixture and mozzarella. Add remaining pasta mixture. Cover with aluminum foil and bake at 375 degrees for 25 minutes.
Uncover and bake 10 more minutes or until bubbly. Remove from the oven and let
stand for about 10 minutes before serving. Serves 8.

EARLY IN DECEMBER I get together with a group of 10 to 15 good friends for an ornament exchange and holiday potluck. Everyone brings a homemade ornament and a tasty dish to share, along with the recipe. It's a wonderful afternoon as we sit around a toasty fire to exchange ornaments, enjoy delicious food and chat about our holiday plans. When the day's over, everyone goes home with several handmade ornaments, new recipes to try and the spirit of Christmas in their hearts.

KATHY FOX
EASTON, MD

Turkey, Almond & Wild Rice Casserole

1 onion, chopped
2 T. butter or margarine
½ c. all-purpose flour
2 (4½-oz.) cans sliced mushrooms, drained and liquid reserved
3 c. half-and-half
½ c. chicken broth
2 c. prepared long-grain and wild rice

6 c. cubed cooked turkey
1 c. slivered almonds, toasted
½ c. diced pimentos
Salt and pepper to taste
¼ c. butter or margarine, melted
1 c. dry bread crumbs
¼ c. chopped fresh parsley

Sauté onion in butter in a saucepan over medium heat; remove from heat and stir in flour. Set aside.

Combine reserved mushroom liquid with half-and-half and enough broth to make 4 cups. Gradually stir into flour mixture; cook, stirring until thickened. Add rice, mushrooms, turkey, toasted almonds, pimentos, salt and pepper. Place in a lightly greased 13"x9" baking dish; set aside. Combine butter, bread crumbs and parsley; sprinkle over top of casserole. Bake, uncovered, at 350 degrees for 40 minutes. Serves 6 to 8.

Weekend Beef Burgundy

(pictured on page 70)

2 lbs. cubed stew beef
2 (10¾-oz.) cans cream of mushroom soup
2.4-oz. pkg. herb and garlic soup mix
1 small onion, chopped

1 t. beef bouillon granules
2 (4½-oz.) cans sliced mushrooms, drained
1 c. Burgundy wine or beef broth
6 c. cooked egg noodles

Combine first 5 ingredients in a large bowl; mix well. Spread mixture in a lightly greased 13"x9" baking dish; bake, covered, at 325 degrees for 2 hours. Add mushrooms and wine; bake 10 more minutes. Serve over noodles. Serves 8 to 10.

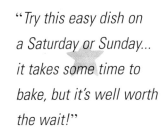

"Try this easy dish on a Saturday or Sunday... it takes some time to bake, but it's well worth the wait!"

VIRGINIA WATSON
SCRANTON, PA

Anytime Enchurritos

2 c. shredded cooked turkey
1½ c. salsa, divided
8-oz. container sour cream
2 to 3 T. diced green chilies
6 (8") flour tortillas

10¾-oz. can cream of chicken soup
2 c. shredded Mexican-blend cheese
Toppings: shredded lettuce, chopped tomatoes (optional)

Combine turkey, ½ cup salsa, sour cream and chilies. Spoon turkey mixture into tortillas; roll up and place seam-side down in an ungreased 13"x9" baking dish. Blend together soup and remaining salsa; pour over tortillas. Bake, uncovered, at 350 degrees for 30 minutes. Sprinkle with cheese and bake 5 more minutes or until cheese is melted. Top with shredded lettuce and chopped tomatoes, if desired. Serves 6 to 8.

Nutty Pudding Cake

18¼-oz. pkg. yellow cake mix
4 (3.5-oz.) cups butterscotch pudding
2 eggs

⅓ c. sugar
1 c. butterscotch chips
1 c. sliced almonds

Combine first 3 ingredients in a bowl; spread in a greased and floured 13"x9" pan. Sprinkle top with sugar, butterscotch chips and almonds; bake at 375 degrees for 28 minutes or until a wooden toothpick inserted in center comes out clean. Serves 10 to 12.

CHRISTMAS IS A VERY SPECIAL TIME OF YEAR FOR MY FAMILY. For two complete days, we get to spend almost every waking moment together. Over the years my grandmother kept a journal of our Christmas celebrations. She wrote down what we ate, what went on, what time Santa Claus arrived and even that special toy all the children loved. This past Christmas we received the best Christmas present ever. She gave each family a personal copy of our memories...so many things happened that we had almost forgotten. We were so thrilled by this sweet book of memories and will continue to add to it each year.

NICOLE ANDERSON
WARREN, OH

Anytime
Enchurritos

Buttermilk
Pound Cake

Buttermilk Pound Cake

½ c. butter or margarine, softened
½ c. shortening
2 c. sugar
4 eggs
½ t. baking soda
1 c. buttermilk

3 c. all-purpose flour
⅛ t. salt
2 t. lemon extract
1 t. almond extract
Fresh strawberries

Beat butter and shortening at medium speed with an electric mixer 2 minutes or until creamy. Gradually add sugar, beating 5 to 7 minutes. Add eggs, one at a time, beating just until yellow disappears.

Dissolve soda in buttermilk. Combine flour and salt; add to butter mixture alternately with buttermilk, beginning and ending with flour mixture. Beat at low speed after each addition just until blended; stir in flavorings.

Pour batter into a greased and floured 10" tube pan. Bake at 350 degrees for one hour or until a wooden toothpick inserted in center comes out clean. Cool in pan on a wire rack 10 to 15 minutes; remove from pan and cool completely on a wire rack. Garnish with fresh strawberries. Serves 14.

THE DAY AFTER THANKSGIVING, I welcomed the holiday season in with a unique celebration. Instead of my usual weekly "girls-night-out," I opted for a "girls-night-in" and hosted a Potpourri-Making Party. I asked each person to bring two ingredients...one purchased and one found around the house or yard. Each was also asked to bring a special treat in the form of food or drink to share with the group. We had a fire, drank champagne, nibbled on shrimp, laughed, told stories and had a great time while we mixed up two huge bowls of Christmas and Kitchen potpourris. Everyone left the party with generous samples of each potpourri to use themselves or to give as gifts. I think they also left feeling a little pampered before the holiday season began. *Joanne Martin-Robinson*

Store-bought items to choose:
- **cinnamon sticks**
- **cinnamon oil**
- **bay leaves**
- **rosemary**
- **ground orris root**
- **whole allspice**
- **whole nutmeg**
- **star anise**
- **lemon balm**
- **balsam or fir oil**

Things found around the house:
- **orange, lemon and lime peels**
- **homegrown herbs & spices**
- **dried apple & orange slices**
- **large pinecone chunks**
- **tiny pinecones**
- **pine needles**
- **holly berries**
- **cranberries**
- **bayberry**
- **juniper**
- **cedar**
- **boxwood**

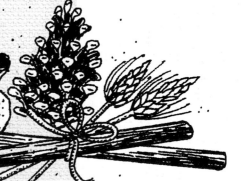

Grapefruit Margaritas (page 85),
Sassy Shrimp (page 93) and Roasted
Red Pepper Bruschetta (page 89)

Christmas
open house

Open your home to family & friends during the holidays

for good cheer, merry treats and festive fun. Sweet-tart sips

of Grapefruit Margaritas and savory bites of appetizers, such as

Crab Rangoon and Roasted Red Pepper Bruschetta, will encourage your

guests to linger as you celebrate this merry season together.

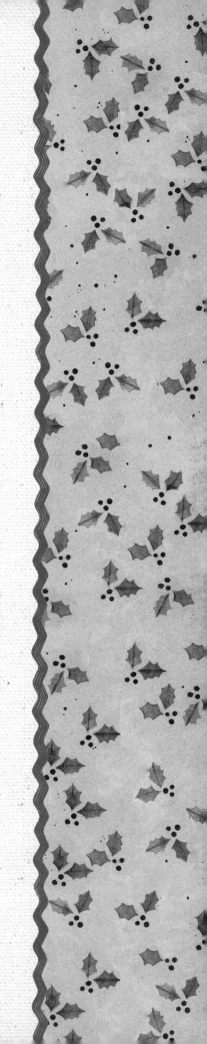

Cinnamon Hot Chocolate

¼ c. baking cocoa
¼ c. sugar
1 c. boiling water

3 c. milk
1 cinnamon stick
1 t. vanilla extract

Add a scoop of ice cream to your favorite hot chocolate. Then top with whipped cream, add a cinnamon stick and sprinkle some chocolate curls on top. Totally yummy!

Combine cocoa and sugar in a heavy saucepan. Slowly add boiling water; bring to a boil and boil for 2 minutes. Add milk and cinnamon stick. Reduce heat and simmer for 10 minutes. Remove cinnamon stick and add vanilla; stir quickly to froth milk. Makes 4 cups.

Cranberry Hot Toddies

16-oz. can jellied cranberry sauce
⅓ c. light brown sugar, packed
¼ t. ground cinnamon
¼ t. ground allspice
⅛ t. ground nutmeg

⅛ t. ground cloves
⅛ t. salt
2 c. water
2 c. pineapple juice
2 T. butter or margarine, sliced

Empty cranberry sauce into a large saucepan. Whisk in sugar and seasonings; add water and pineapple juice. Cover and simmer for about 2 hours. Pour into mugs and top each mug with a pat of butter. Makes 6 cups.

Spiced Hot Buttered Rum Punch

½ c. butter or margarine, softened
½ c. brown sugar, packed
½ t. ground cloves
½ t. ground cinnamon

½ t. vanilla extract
3½ c. boiling water
1¼ c. spiced rum
Garnish: 3" cinnamon sticks

Pull out your favorite holiday mugs and a jar of cinnamon sticks for this classic. Small servings will warm your guests nicely.

Combine first 5 ingredients in a small bowl, stirring until smooth. Cover and chill until ready to serve.

To serve, combine butter mixture, boiling water, and rum in a small punch bowl, stirring until butter mixture melts. Serve warm with cinnamon-stick stirrers, if desired. Makes 5½ cups.

Spiced Coffee-Eggnog Punch

2 c. strong brewed coffee
1½ (3") cinnamon sticks
6 whole allspice
6 whole cloves
2 (32-oz.) cans eggnog, chilled

1 T. vanilla extract
1 c. whipping cream, whipped
1 qt. vanilla ice cream, softened
Ground nutmeg

Combine first 4 ingredients in a saucepan. Bring to a boil; reduce heat and simmer, uncovered, for 15 minutes. Pour coffee mixture through a wire-mesh strainer into a bowl, discarding spices; chill.

Combine coffee mixture, eggnog and vanilla in a large bowl; fold in whipped cream. Spoon softened ice cream into a punch bowl. Pour eggnog mixture over ice cream and stir gently. Sprinkle punch with ground nutmeg. Makes 11 cups.

Apple-Cinnamon Punch

1 c. water
½ c. sugar
½ c. red cinnamon candies

2 (2-ltr.) bottles raspberry ginger ale, chilled
46-oz. can apple juice, chilled

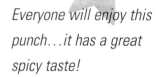

Everyone will enjoy this punch...it has a great spicy taste!

Combine water, sugar and candies in a small saucepan; bring to a boil. Reduce heat and simmer, uncovered, for 5 minutes or until candies melt; stir occasionally. When mixture has cooled, combine with ginger ale and apple juice; stir well. Makes 25 cups.

Grapefruit Margaritas

(pictured on page 82)

6-oz. can frozen limeade concentrate
⅔ c. ruby red grapefruit juice
⅔ c. white tequila

¼ c. orange liqueur
Sparkling sugar

If you want slushy margaritas for a crowd, make several batches in advance and freeze until ready to serve. There's no need to thaw them; just stir and serve.

Combine first 4 ingredients in an electric blender, adding crushed ice to 5-cup level; process just until slushy. Pour into a pitcher and serve immediately, or cover and freeze. To serve, wet the rims of stemmed glasses and dip in sparkling sugar. Makes 3½ cups.

Cheddar Fondue

¼ c. butter
¼ c. all-purpose flour
½ t. salt
¼ t. pepper

¼ t. dry mustard
¼ t. Worcestershire sauce
1½ c. milk
2 c. (8 oz.) shredded Cheddar cheese

Melt butter in a saucepan. Whisk in flour, salt, pepper, mustard and Worcestershire sauce until smooth; gradually add milk. Bring to a boil; cook 2 minutes or until thickened, stirring often. Reduce heat; add cheese, stirring until melted. Transfer to fondue pot or slow cooker to keep warm. Makes 2½ cups.

Christmas Brie

8-oz. pkg. Brie cheese
½ c. sun-dried tomatoes, minced
½ c. minced fresh parsley

5 cloves garlic, minced
2 T. olive oil

Carefully remove and discard the rind from top of cheese; set cheese aside. Combine tomatoes and remaining 3 ingredients in a microwave-safe bowl; microwave on HIGH (100%) for 2 to 3 minutes or until garlic has softened. Spread over top of cheese; microwave on HIGH for 45 seconds or until cheese melts. Serves 6 to 8.

Chunky Gorgonzola Dip

8-oz. carton mascarpone cheese
⅓ c. sour cream
⅓ c. chopped fresh chives
½ t. salt

¼ t. ground white pepper
4 oz. Gorgonzola cheese, crumbled
Garnish: chopped fresh chives

Combine mascarpone cheese and sour cream in a small bowl; stir with a wooden spoon until smooth. Stir in chives, salt and pepper. Gently stir in Gorgonzola cheese, leaving dip chunky. Garnish, if desired. Serve dip with sliced apples and pears, crackers and toasted walnuts. Makes 2 cups.

Cheddar Fondue

Florentine
Artichoke Dip

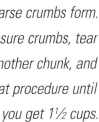

To get 1½ cups French bread crumbs for this recipe, tear off a piece of a baguette. Pulse in a food processor until coarse crumbs form. Measure crumbs, tear off another chunk, and repeat procedure until you get 1½ cups.

Florentine Artichoke Dip

10-oz. pkg. frozen chopped spinach, thawed
12-oz. jar marinated artichoke hearts, drained and chopped
1½ (8-oz.) pkgs. cream cheese, softened
1 c. freshly shredded Parmesan cheese
½ c. mayonnaise
3 large cloves garlic, pressed
2 T. lemon juice
1½ c. French bread crumbs (homemade)
2 T. butter or margarine, melted

Drain spinach; press between layers of paper towels to remove excess moisture.

Combine spinach, artichoke hearts and next 5 ingredients in a bowl, stirring well. Spoon into a lightly greased 11"x7" baking dish. Combine bread crumbs and butter; sprinkle over spinach mixture.

Bake, uncovered, at 375 degrees for 25 minutes. Serve with assorted crackers, bagel chips or breadsticks. Makes 4 cups.

Smoky Nuts

¼ c. honey
2 T. sugar
2 T. chipotle peppers with 1 t. pepper
   liquid, puréed

1½ c. pecan halves
1½ c. whole almonds
Salt

Instead of using both pecans and almonds, you can also use 3 cups of any one type of nut for this recipe.

Combine first 3 ingredients in a medium saucepan. Cook over medium heat until sugar dissolves, stirring often. Stir in nuts.

Spread coated nuts in a single layer in a lightly greased 15"x10" jelly roll pan. Bake at 300 degrees for 20 minutes; stir and bake 10 to 15 more minutes. Spread warm nuts onto aluminum foil or parchment paper; separate nuts with a fork. Lightly sprinkle with salt; cool. Store nuts between layers of parchment paper or wax paper in an airtight container up to 3 days. Makes 3½ cups.

Roasted Red Pepper Bruschetta

(pictured on page 82)

12-oz. jar roasted red bell peppers,
   drained well and finely chopped
½ c. finely chopped plum tomato
¼ c. finely chopped red onion
2 T. balsamic vinegar
2 T. olive oil
½ t. salt
½ t. freshly ground pepper

Dash of sugar
1 baguette, cut diagonally into
   24 slices
¼ c. olive oil
Salt and pepper
½ c. crumbled garlic and herb-
   flavored feta cheese

Combine first 3 ingredients in a bowl. Combine vinegar, 2 tablespoons olive oil, ½ teaspoon salt, ½ teaspoon pepper and sugar; pour over pepper mixture and toss well. Cover and chill until ready to serve.

Arrange baguette slices on a large ungreased baking sheet. Brush or drizzle slices with ¼ cup oil; sprinkle with salt and pepper. Bake at 400 degrees for 4 minutes or until barely toasted.

Spoon about one tablespoon roasted pepper mixture onto each toast; top each with crumbled feta. Broil 5½ inches from heat 3 minutes or until bubbly and barely browned. Serve warm. Makes 2 dozen.

Cranberry Meatballs

2 lbs. ground beef
1 t. parsley flakes
2 T. soy sauce
½ t. garlic salt
2 T. chopped onion

1 c. uncooked quick-cooking oats
2 eggs, beaten
¼ t. pepper
⅓ c. catsup

Combine all ingredients in a large bowl. Roll into 2-inch balls; arrange in a shallow baking pan. Bake at 350 degrees for 25 minutes; drain. Spoon Sauce over meatballs and bake 15 more minutes. Makes 42 meatballs.

Sauce

16-oz. can jellied cranberry sauce
12-oz. bottle chili sauce

½ c. brown sugar, packed
1 T. lemon juice

Whisk together all ingredients in a medium bowl. Makes 3 cups.

Hot Antipasto Squares

2 (8-oz.) cans crescent rolls, divided
¼ lb. thinly sliced cooked ham
¼ lb. thinly sliced Swiss cheese
¼ lb. thinly sliced salami
¼ lb. thinly sliced provolone cheese

¼ lb. thinly sliced pepperoni
2 eggs, beaten
7-oz. jar roasted red bell peppers,
    drained and chopped
3 T. grated Parmesan cheese

Unroll one can of crescent rolls; press into an ungreased 13"x9" pan, sealing edges. Layer the meats and cheeses in the order given; lightly press down. Combine eggs, peppers and Parmesan cheese in a small mixing bowl; pour over pepperoni layer. Unroll remaining crescent rolls; shape into a 13"x9" rectangle, pressing seams together gently. Carefully place on top of the egg mixture. Bake at 375 degrees for 30 minutes. Cool; cut into one-inch squares to serve. Makes about 5 dozen.

CLEVER PARTY FAVORS Purchase mini candy canes in the long, clear cellophane wrappers (the kind that are usually hanging on display racks). Tie on red and green bows between the candy canes. Hang them on the wall by your front door, along with a small pair of scissors. As guests leave, cut off a candy cane for them to take with them. You can also do this with small homemade gingerbread men. Simply wrap them in a long strip of plastic wrap.   LISA GLENN

Cranberry Meatballs

Chicken Fingers with Apple Butter-Peanut Sauce

1 lb. skinned and boned chicken breasts
¼ c. all-purpose flour
1 t. salt
½ t. pepper
1 egg, beaten

⅓ c. milk
½ c. Italian-seasoned bread crumbs
¼ c. sesame seeds
¼ t. salt
3 T. butter or margarine, melted
Apple Butter-Peanut Sauce

Cut chicken into ¼-inch lengthwise strips. Combine flour, one teaspoon salt and pepper in a large zip-top plastic bag. Add chicken strips, seal bag and shake to coat.

Combine egg and milk in a shallow dish, stirring well. Combine bread crumbs, sesame seeds and ¼ teaspoon salt in a shallow dish. Dip chicken strips in egg mixture and dredge in bread crumb mixture. Place in a lightly greased 13"x9" baking dish; drizzle with butter.

Cover and bake at 425 degrees for 20 minutes; uncover and bake 18 to 20 more minutes or until done. Serve with Apple Butter-Peanut Sauce, using short wooden skewers. Makes 10 appetizer servings.

Apple Butter-Peanut Sauce

½ c. creamy peanut butter
⅓ c. apple butter
1¼ c. chicken broth

1 T. freshly grated ginger
¼ t. salt

Combine all ingredients in a small saucepan over medium-high heat. Bring just to a boil; reduce heat and simmer, uncovered, 2 minutes or until thickened, stirring constantly. Remove from heat; cool. Serve at room temperature. Makes 1¾ cups.

MY FAMILY ARE CHRISTMAS CRAZIES! We start celebrating the Saturday after Thanksgiving by writing out our Christmas cards. We then have a party every weekend until Christmas. All the parties have a theme and we even give away door prizes! Last year we had a snowflake card party and decorated old mailboxes to store our cards in. In the past we have each decorated a door in my grandparents' house! The season doesn't end until New Year's Eve with a movie, game playing and pizza party. We are a family of 25 and every Christmas Eve is spent at my grandparents' house. All of this started when my husband and I first married and had our first child. Money was tight and we couldn't afford a lot of decorations. The relatives showed up and we created homemade decorations… paper chains and popcorn strings!

VIRGINIA HAGERMAN
JOLO, WV

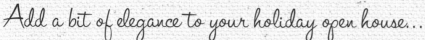
Crab Rangoon

8 oz. pasteurized crabmeat
12 oz. cream cheese, softened
¼ t. garlic powder
¼ t. seasoned salt

16-oz. pkg. won ton wrappers
  (3½" squares)
Oil for deep-frying

Combine first 4 ingredients in a medium bowl; mix well. Spoon about 2 teaspoons crab mixture into the center of each won ton; brush edges with water. Fold and pinch corners, completely enclosing filling.

Pour oil into a Dutch oven, filling at least half full; heat to 350 degrees over medium-high heat. Fry won tons, in batches, in hot oil 2 to 3 minutes or until golden. Drain on paper towels; serve immediately. Makes about 4 dozen.

"Serve these yummy appetizers by themselves or with your favorite dipping sauce, such as duck or plum sauce. They're also great with your favorite chicken dish!"

SUSIE BACKUS
GOOSEBERRY PATCH

Sassy Shrimp

(pictured on page 82)

6 c. water
2 lbs. unpeeled, medium-size fresh
  shrimp
½ c. lemon juice
¼ c. vegetable oil
2 cloves garlic, crushed
1 bay leaf, crumbled
1 T. dry mustard
1 T. red wine vinegar

2 t. salt
½ t. paprika
Dash of ground red pepper
3¼-oz. can whole pitted ripe olives,
  drained
1 medium-size red onion, thinly sliced
1 lemon, thinly sliced
2-oz. jar diced pimentos, drained
2 T. chopped fresh parsley

Bring water to a boil; add shrimp and cook 3 to 5 minutes or until shrimp turn pink. Drain well; rinse with cold water. Peel shrimp and devein, if desired. Set aside.

Combine lemon juice and next 8 ingredients in a large bowl; stir with a wire whisk until blended. Add olives, onion, lemon, pimentos and parsley; stir well. Add shrimp; toss to coat. Cover and marinate in refrigerator one to 4 hours. Makes 8 appetizer servings.

Cream Cheese
Scrambled Eggs
(page 103),
Pears with Cranberry
Relish (page 97),
Crispy Brown Sugar
Bacon (page 100)
and Sunshine in a
Glass (page 96)

Breakfasts & brunches

Rise and shine to the cinnamon aroma of Hot Percolator Punch.

If that doesn't get you going then try a slice of hearty Savory Ham-and-Swiss

Breakfast Pie or nibble on a slice of Simple Citrus Coffee Cake. Whether

you're hosting a brunch or serving breakfast on Christmas morning, these

eye-opening selections are guaranteed to jump-start your day.

Hot Percolator Punch

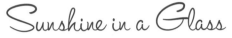

3 c. unsweetened pineapple juice
3 c. cranberry-apple juice drink
1 c. water
⅓ c. light brown sugar, packed

2 lemon slices
2 (4") cinnamon sticks, broken
1½ t. whole cloves
Additional cinnamon sticks (optional)

Pour juices and water into a 12-cup percolator. Place brown sugar and next 3 ingredients in percolator basket. Perk through complete cycle of electric percolator. Serve with cinnamon sticks as stirrers, if desired. Makes 7 cups.

Sunshine in a Glass

(pictured on page 94)

1 c. frozen orange juice concentrate,
    partially thawed
½ c. milk

10 to 12 ice cubes
1 t. vanilla extract

Place ingredients in an electric blender; blend until smooth. Makes 2½ cups.

Hot Vanilla

1 c. milk
1 t. honey

⅛ t. vanilla extract
⅛ t. ground cinnamon

Heat milk until very hot but not boiling in a saucepan. Pour milk into a mug. Add honey, vanilla and cinnamon. Mix well and serve immediately. Makes one cup.

Warm Spiced Fruit

20-oz. plus 8-oz. cans pineapple
    chunks, juice reserved
29-oz. can sliced peaches, drained
29-oz. can pear halves, quartered and
    drained

¾ c. brown sugar, packed
¼ c. butter or margarine
2 (3") cinnamon sticks
½ t. ground ginger

Combine pineapple, peaches and pears; spoon into a 3½-quart baking dish. Stir together brown sugar, butter, cinnamon, ginger and reserved pineapple juice in a saucepan; bring to a boil. Reduce heat and simmer 5 minutes; discard cinnamon sticks. Pour juice over fruit and bake, uncovered, at 350 degrees for 30 minutes or until heated through. Serves 10 to 12.

Pears with Cranberry Relish

(pictured on page 94)

2 large Braeburn apples, cored and
    quartered
12-oz. pkg. fresh cranberries
1 lemon, quartered and seeded

1½ c. sugar
8 Bartlett pears, halved lengthwise
    and cored

Process apples in a food processor until well chopped; remove and place in a medium bowl. Add cranberries and lemon to food processor and process until well chopped; stir into apples. Add sugar, stirring well. Cover and chill 2 to 3 hours.

Spoon relish into the pears and serve immediately. Serves 16.

A melon baller or grapefruit spoon is a great tool to use when removing the core from halved pears.

Can't-Fail Biscuits

2 c. self-rising flour

1 c. whipping cream

Mix together flour and whipping cream (dough will be stiff). Turn dough out onto a lightly floured surface and knead 10 to 12 times.

Roll dough to ½-inch thickness; cut with a 2-inch biscuit cutter. Place on a lightly greased baking sheet; bake at 450 degrees for 10 to 12 minutes or until lightly browned. Makes about one dozen.

"A really easy biscuit recipe. Tasty when spread with jams or honey."

ARLENE GRIMM
DECATUR, AL

Chocolate Gravy for Biscuits

2½ c. sugar
¼ c. all-purpose flour
¼ c. baking cocoa

3 c. milk
1 t. vanilla extract
1 T. butter

Bring sugar, flour, cocoa and milk to a boil in a large saucepan. Reduce heat and simmer for 13 minutes or until thick and bubbly, stirring every 2 to 3 minutes. Stir in vanilla and butter. Serve over warm biscuits. Makes 4½ cups.

WE VISIT MY HUSBAND'S AUNT IN GEORGIA EVERY CHRISTMAS SEASON. Biscuits with Chocolate Gravy is one of my favorite memories. This recipe has been a tradition in my husband's family for at least 4 generations now! The men like it so much that they put the chocolate gravy over everything...eggs, bacon, sausage and pancakes.

KELLY SUMMERS
JEFFERSON, OH

Cheese Biscuits

2 c. self-rising flour
1 t. dry mustard
6 T. shortening

1 c. (4 oz.) shredded sharp Cheddar
   cheese
¾ c. buttermilk

Stir together flour and mustard; cut in shortening with a pastry blender until mixture is crumbly. Stir in cheese. Add buttermilk, stirring until dry ingredients are moistened. Turn dough out onto a lightly floured surface and knead 3 or 4 times.

Roll dough to ¾-inch thickness; cut with a 2-inch biscuit cutter. Place biscuits on a lightly greased baking sheet. Bake at 450 degrees for 10 to 12 minutes or until lightly browned. Makes one dozen.

A little mustard boosts the cheese flavor in these quick biscuits. To get a head start, grate the cheese the night before.

Sour Cream Twists

"My mom used to greet me at the door with these when I came home from school, but they're perfect anytime!"

EMILY FLAKE
COLORADO SPRINGS, CO

¼-oz. pkg. active dry yeast
¼ c. warm water (100 degrees to 110
   degrees)
1 c. shortening, melted
8-oz. container sour cream
1 t. salt
1 t. vanilla extract
2 eggs

3½ c. all-purpose flour
1 c. granulated sugar
1 t. ground cinnamon
2 c. powdered sugar
2 t. vanilla extract
½ c. butter, melted
2 T. heavy whipping cream

Combine yeast and water in a small bowl; let stand 5 minutes.

Combine shortening, sour cream, salt and vanilla in a medium bowl; stir in yeast mixture and eggs. Stir in flour and mix well. Cover and chill 2 hours.

Combine granulated sugar and cinnamon in a small bowl. Roll out dough on a lightly floured surface into a 15"x10" rectangle. Sprinkle dough with ⅓ cup cinnamon-sugar mixture. Fold rectangle in thirds, like a letter. Roll dough into another 15"x10" rectangle; sprinkle with ⅓ cup cinnamon-sugar mixture. Fold rectangle into thirds again. Repeat entire procedure one more time, finishing with a 15"x10" rectangle. Cut final rectangle into 4"x1" strips; twist 2 times.

Place twists one-inch apart on greased baking sheets; bake at 400 degrees for 10 minutes.

Combine powdered sugar and remaining 3 ingredients, stirring well; drizzle glaze over warm twists. Makes about 4 dozen.

Blueberry-Croissant
French Toast

Blueberry-Croissant French Toast

1 c. half-and-half
2 eggs
⅓ c. granulated sugar
¼ c. milk
1 t. ground cinnamon
¼ t. salt

8 T. blueberry preserves, divided
4 croissants, sliced horizontally
½ c. butter or margarine
2 c. blueberries
Toppings: maple syrup, powdered
    sugar

Combine first 6 ingredients in a bowl. Pour mixture into a 13"x9" baking dish; set aside.

Spread 2 tablespoons preserves on each of 4 croissant halves; top with remaining halves. Arrange croissants on top of egg mixture; turn to coat. Set aside until liquid is absorbed, about 45 minutes; turn often.

Melt ¼ cup butter in a 12" skillet over medium heat; add 2 croissants and cook until golden on both sides. Transfer croissants to serving plates and keep warm. Wipe skillet clean; repeat with remaining ¼ cup butter and 2 croissants. Add blueberries to skillet; cook for 3½ minutes or until heated thoroughly. Spoon berries over croissants; serve with desired toppings. Serves 4.

"Enjoy this simple twist on a favorite breakfast classic."

JO ANN

Simple Citrus Coffee Cake

¼-oz. pkg. active dry yeast
½ c. warm water (100 degrees to 110 degrees)
½ c. all-purpose flour
1 c. light brown sugar, packed
1 T. ground cinnamon
¼ c. butter, softened

18¼-oz. pkg. white cake mix
3 eggs
¼ c. orange juice
2 T. butter, melted
1 c. powdered sugar
½ t. grated orange zest
2 T. orange juice

Combine yeast and warm water in a one-cup glass measuring cup; let stand 5 minutes.

Meanwhile combine flour, brown sugar and cinnamon. Cut in ¼ cup butter with a pastry blender or 2 forks until mixture resembles cornmeal; set aside.

Combine yeast mixture, cake mix and next 3 ingredients in a large mixing bowl; beat at low speed with an electric mixer just until moistened. Beat at medium speed 2 more minutes.

Pour half the batter into a greased and floured 12-cup Bundt® pan. Sprinkle brown sugar mixture over batter. Top with remaining batter.

Bake at 350 degrees for 35 minutes or until a wooden toothpick inserted in center comes out almost clean. Cool in pan on a wire rack 15 minutes; remove from pan and cool 15 minutes or until cake is just warm.

Combine powdered sugar, orange zest and 2 tablespoons orange juice, stirring until smooth; drizzle over cake. Serve warm. Serves 12 to 15.

Crispy Brown Sugar Bacon

(pictured on page 94)

1 lb. thick sliced hickory-smoked bacon slices

1 c. light brown sugar, packed
1 T. cracked black pepper

Cut bacon slices in half. Combine sugar and pepper in a shallow dish. Dredge bacon in sugar mixture, shaking off excess. Twist each bacon slice, if desired.

Place bacon in a single layer on a lightly greased baking rack in an aluminum foil-lined baking pan. Bake at 425 degrees for 20 to 25 minutes or until crisp. Allow bacon to cool before serving. Serves 6.

Family coming for a holiday brunch?

Copy one of Grandma's tried & true recipes onto a festive card, then punch a hole in the corner and tie the card to a napkin with a length of ribbon...a sweet keepsake.

Simple Citrus
Coffee Cake

Savory Ham-and-Swiss Breakfast Pie

1⅔ c. water
1 c. whipping cream
2 cloves garlic, pressed
2 T. butter or margarine
1 t. salt
¼ t. pepper
⅔ c. uncooked quick-cooking grits

1¼ c. (5 oz.) shredded Swiss cheese, divided
8 eggs, divided
½ lb. cooked ham, diced
4 green onions, chopped
½ c. milk
Garnish: fresh chives

Bring first 6 ingredients to a boil in a saucepan; gradually whisk in grits. Cover, reduce heat and simmer 5 to 7 minutes, whisking occasionally. Add ½ cup cheese, stirring until cheese melts. Remove from heat; let stand 10 minutes. Lightly beat 2 eggs and stir into grits mixture; pour into a greased 10" deep-dish pie plate.

Bake at 350 degrees for 20 minutes; remove from oven. Increase temperature to 400 degrees.

Sauté ham and onions in a nonstick skillet over medium-high heat 5 minutes or until onion is tender. Layer ham mixture evenly over grits crust. Whisk together milk and remaining 6 eggs; pour over ham mixture. Sprinkle remaining ¾ cup cheese evenly over egg mixture.

Bake at 400 degrees for 35 minutes. Let stand 10 minutes and cut into wedges. Garnish, if desired. Serves 8.

Cream Cheese Scrambled Eggs

(pictured on page 94)

12 eggs
1 c. half-and-half or milk
2 (3-oz.) pkgs. cream cheese, cubed
¾ t. salt

¼ t. pepper
¼ c. butter or margarine
Chopped fresh chives

Stir the eggs only a few times during cooking. Stirring constantly makes them dry and crumbly.

Process first 5 ingredients in a blender until frothy, stopping to scrape down sides.
Melt butter in a large heavy skillet over medium heat; reduce heat to medium-low. Add egg mixture and cook, without stirring, until mixture begins to set on bottom. Draw a spatula across bottom of skillet to form large curds. Continue cooking until eggs are thickened but still moist; do not stir constantly. Sprinkle with chives. Serves 6 to 8.

Sausage-Filled Crêpes

1 lb. ground sausage, browned
¼ c. diced onion
1½ c. shredded American cheese
3-oz. pkg. cream cheese, softened
3 eggs, beaten
1 c. milk

1 T. vegetable oil
1 T. water
1 c. all-purpose flour
½ t. salt
½ c. sour cream
¼ c. butter or margarine, softened

"Enjoy a glass of freshly squeezed orange juice with these savory crêpes!"

Renae Reu
Luverne, MN

Combine first 4 ingredients until blended; set aside. Whisk together eggs, milk, oil and water. Stir in flour and salt. Lightly grease a 7" skillet and place over medium-high heat. Add 3 tablespoons of batter to pan; quickly tilt to coat bottom. Cook 3 minutes or until edges are golden and lift easily. Turn and cook 3 minutes. Repeat procedure with remaining batter. Place 3 tablespoons sausage mixture down the center of each crêpe; roll up and place in a greased 13"x9" baking dish. Bake, uncovered, at 375 degrees for 20 minutes. Combine sour cream and butter; spoon over crêpes. Bake, uncovered, 5 minutes. Serves 9.

Creamy Crab Bake

1 lb. lump crabmeat, shell pieces
   removed
8-oz. pkg. shredded sharp Cheddar
   cheese
2 c. seasoned croutons
2 c. milk

2 eggs, lightly beaten
1 T. dried, minced onion
1 T. dried parsley
½ t. salt
¼ t. pepper
¼ c. grated fresh Parmesan cheese

Combine first 9 ingredients in a bowl. Spoon into a lightly greased 11"x7" baking dish; sprinkle with Parmesan cheese. Bake, uncovered, at 325 degrees for 50 minutes or until a knife inserted into the center comes out clean. Serves 8.

White Chicken Chili
(page 112)

Heartwarming Soups & stews

Soup's on and it's never been tastier! For a crowd, ladle up bowls

full of White Chicken Chili…it makes over 20 cups! Or snuggle in on a cold

evening with Cream of Tomato Soup and grilled cheese sandwiches. Whether

you're serving a big group or just your family, these soups & stews

deliver comfort for the appetite and the soul.

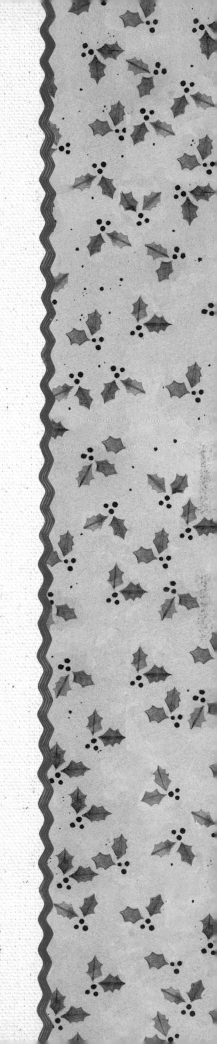

This fancy bisque is laced with chunks of savory lobster, flavored with sherry and thickened with cream for a velvety taste and texture.

Lobster & Chive Bisque

3 T. butter
1 T. minced onion
3 T. all-purpose flour
3 c. milk
1 c. heavy whipping cream

½ c. dry sherry
1 t. salt
⅛ t. paprika
1 c. cooked lobster (about 5 oz.)
2 T. chopped fresh chives

Melt butter in a Dutch oven over medium heat; add onion and sauté one minute or until tender. Add flour, stirring until blended. Cook one minute, stirring constantly. Gradually add milk and next 4 ingredients. Bring just to a simmer; cook, uncovered, 5 minutes or until slightly thickened (do not boil). Stir in lobster and chives. Makes 5 cups.

Bistro Onion Soup

4 large onions (about 2 pounds), sliced
¼ c. butter or margarine, melted
2 T. all-purpose flour
5¼ c. water
½ c. dry white wine
½ c. dry red wine
4 chicken bouillon cubes

4 beef bouillon cubes
2 bay leaves
½ t. salt
½ t. dried sage
¼ t. pepper
8 (½") diagonally sliced French bread slices, toasted
8 slices Gruyère cheese

Sauté onion in butter in a Dutch oven over medium heat 15 minutes or until golden, stirring often. Stir in flour; cook one minute. Add water and next 8 ingredients. Bring to a boil; reduce heat and simmer, partially covered, 30 minutes. Discard bay leaves.

Ladle soup into 4 individual oven-proof soup bowls. Place on a baking sheet. Add 2 bread slices to each bowl and cover with 2 slices cheese. Broil 5½ inches from heat 2 minutes or until cheese is bubbly. Serve immediately. Makes 6 cups.

Note: Equal amounts of chicken broth and beef broth can be substituted for the white and red wine but omit the ½ teaspoon of salt.

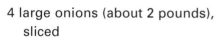

There's nothing more cozy than a bowl of warm soup.

For extra comfort, warm up oven-safe bowls in a 200-degree oven before filling... the soup (and the guests) will stay warmer longer!

Bistro
Onion Soup

Baked Potato Soup

This family-pleaser is the popular loaded & stuffed baked potato... soup style!

Baked Potato Soup

4 large baking potatoes
⅔ c. butter or margarine
⅔ c. all-purpose flour
7 c. milk
4 green onions, sliced
12-oz. pkg. bacon, cooked and crumbled

1¼ c. (5 oz.) shredded Cheddar cheese
8-oz. container sour cream
¾ t. salt
½ t. pepper
Garnish: additional shredded Cheddar cheese, cooked and crumbled bacon, sliced green onions

Bake potatoes at 400 degrees for one hour or until done; cool. Cut potatoes in half lengthwise; scoop out pulp and reserve. Discard shells.

Melt butter in a Dutch oven over low heat. Whisk in flour until smooth. Cook one minute, stirring constantly. Gradually whisk in milk; cook over medium heat 10 minutes, whisking constantly, until mixture is thickened and bubbly.

Stir in potato pulp and green onions; bring to a boil. Cover, reduce heat and simmer 10 minutes. Add bacon and next 4 ingredients; stir until cheese melts. Garnish, if desired. Serve immediately. Makes 14 cups.

Christmas Eve Oyster-Corn Chowder

1 large onion, chopped
2 celery ribs, chopped
¼ c. butter, melted
2 new potatoes, cut into ¼" cubes
2 medium carrots, cut into ¼" slices
¼ c. chopped fresh flat-leaf parsley
3 c. half-and-half, divided

7-oz. can cream-style corn
1 t. salt
½ t. sugar
¼ t. freshly ground pepper
1 to 2 (12-oz.) containers fresh oysters, undrained

Sauté onion and celery in butter in a Dutch oven over medium heat until tender. Add potatoes, carrots and parsley; cook one minute. Add 2 cups half-and-half and bring to a boil. Reduce heat and simmer, uncovered, 15 minutes or until potatoes are tender. Stir in remaining one cup half-and-half, corn and remaining ingredients. Bring to a boil; reduce heat and simmer, uncovered, 5 minutes or until edges of oysters curl. Serve immediately. Makes 8 cups.

Cream of Tomato Soup

3 lbs. plum tomatoes
2 T. butter or margarine
1 onion, coarsely chopped
1 clove garlic, minced
2 T. chopped fresh tarragon leaves
½ t. allspice
½ t. sugar

¼ t. salt
6 c. chicken broth
1 T. tomato paste
1 t. orange zest
1 c. whipping cream
Garnish: fresh chives, snipped

Bring 4 quarts water to a boil in a 6-quart Dutch oven. Cut an "X" in bottom of tomatoes with a small paring knife. Scald tomatoes, about one pound at a time, in hot water one minute or until skins begin to split; plunge into cold water. Drain, peel and coarsely chop.

Melt butter in Dutch oven over medium-low heat. Add onion and cook about 10 minutes or until softened. Add garlic, tarragon, allspice, sugar and salt; cook, stirring for one minute. Add tomatoes, chicken broth and tomato paste to the pot; bring to a boil. Reduce heat to medium, partially cover and simmer for 30 minutes. Stir in orange zest and cool for 20 minutes. Purée the soup, in batches, in a blender or food processor. Return to Dutch oven, stir in cream and heat thoroughly over low heat. Do not boil. Garnish with chives and serve. Makes 11 cups.

"Grilled cheese sandwiches are a must with this creamy soup."

CONNIE BRYANT
TOPEKA, KS

Christmas~ that magic blanket that wraps itself around us....

AUGUSTA RUNDEL

Hearty Ham & Bean Soup

¼ c. dried black beans
¼ c. dried red beans
¼ c. dried pinto beans
¼ c. dried navy beans
¼ c. dried black-eyed peas
¼ c. dried Great Northern beans
¼ c. dried lentils
¼ c. dried split peas
2 qts. water

2 (8-oz.) pkg. diced cooked ham
1 large onion, chopped
1 clove garlic, minced
1 t. salt
14½-oz. can diced tomatoes
10-oz. can tomatoes and green chilies, undrained
¼ c. barley

Sort and wash beans; place in a Dutch oven. Cover with water 2 inches above beans; let soak overnight.

Drain beans. Add water, ham, onion, garlic and salt. Cover and bring to a boil. Reduce heat and simmer 1½ hours or until beans are tender. Add tomatoes and remaining ingredients; simmer 30 minutes, stirring occasionally. Makes 12½ cups.

Chicken Soup with Wild Rice and Mushrooms

2 T. butter or margarine
2 small onions, diced
3 carrots, diced
3 celery ribs, diced
2 cloves garlic, minced
1 c. wild rice, uncooked
8 c. chicken broth

2 bay leaves
1 t. dried thyme
2½ c. chopped cooked chicken
8 oz. pkg. sliced mushrooms
½ c. white wine
½ t. salt
½ t. pepper

Melt butter in a large stockpot; add onions, carrots, celery and garlic. Sauté until vegetables are tender. Add rice, broth and herbs. Simmer, covered, for one hour. Add chicken and remaining ingredients. Discard bay leaves. Makes 12 cups.

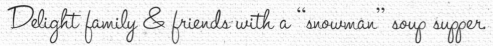

Delight family & friends with a "snowman" soup supper.

Using three plates, place the smallest at the top and largest at the bottom of each place setting. Decorate your snowman "face" with cheese cubes, oyster crackers or croutons; use a roll for his tummy and a bowl of soup for his base.

3-Bean Ravioli Minestrone

3-Bean Ravioli Minestrone

1 T. olive oil
1 onion, chopped
2 carrots, chopped
2 celery ribs, sliced
2 cloves garlic, minced
3 (14-oz.) cans chicken broth
9-oz. pkg. frozen baby lima beans, thawed
16-oz. can light red kidney beans, rinsed and drained

16-oz. can garbanzo beans, rinsed and drained
2 (14½-oz.) cans diced tomatoes
2 t. Italian seasoning
1 t. pepper
½ t. salt
7-oz. pkg. mini cheese ravioli
Shredded Parmesan cheese

Combine first 13 ingredients in a large stockpot. Cover and simmer 30 minutes. Add ravioli and cook 10 minutes or until tender. Serve with shredded fresh Parmesan cheese. Makes 14 cups.

Soup Pointers

• **Make your soups ahead.** Many soups take on a richer flavor if made a day ahead… it gives the flavors time to blend.

• **To remove fat from soups,** either use a bulb baster or wrap an ice cube in damp cheesecloth and skim it over the soup's surface. The fat will firm up on contact and is easily removed. Or cover and chill the soup overnight. The fat will solidify on top and can be lifted off.

• **Soup too salty?** Drop a peeled, raw potato into the pot and let it cook for a few minutes. Remove the potato just before serving the soup.

• **To prevent mushy vegetables,** add the quicker-cooking foods, such as carrots or canned vegetables, after the meat is tender. Cook them until fork-tender, about 15 minutes.

• **To freeze,** package soups & stews in pint or quart plastic freezer containers or heavy-duty plastic freezer bags; label, date and freeze up to 3 months.

*For a heartier soup,
add chopped, cooked
chicken breasts.*

Tortilla Soup

6 (14½-oz.) cans chicken broth
2 (4.5-oz.) cans diced mild green
    chilies, drained
2 cloves garlic, minced
⅓ c. chopped fresh mint
1 t. chili powder
1 t. ground cumin
Red pepper flakes to taste

1 c. chopped tomatoes
2 avocados, pitted, peeled and
    chopped
4 slices bacon, cooked and crumbled
½ c. plus 2 t. chopped fresh cilantro,
    divided
Tortilla chips, slightly crushed
Sour cream

Combine first 7 ingredients in a large Dutch oven; bring to a boil. Cover, reduce heat to low and simmer for about one hour.

Meanwhile, combine tomatoes, avocados, bacon and ½ cup cilantro in a small bowl. To serve, ladle broth into individual soup bowls; place a scoopful of tomato mixture onto each and top with tortilla chips, sour cream and remaining cilantro. Serve immediately. Makes 12 cups.

*"Try lime-flavored
tortilla chips with this
soup... yummy!"*

SUSAN NAFZIGER
CANTON, KS

Taco Soup

1½ lbs. ground chuck
1 medium onion, chopped
1.25-oz. pkg. taco seasoning
1-oz. pkg. Ranch dressing mix
1 c. water
16-oz. pkg. frozen corn

16-oz. can kidney beans, undrained
15-oz. can tomato sauce
14.5-oz. can diced tomatoes with
    green chilies, undrained
Toppings: corn chips, shredded
    Cheddar cheese, sour cream

Cook ground chuck and onion in a stockpot, stirring until beef crumbles and is no longer pink; drain. Add taco seasoning and next 6 ingredients to beef mixture. Bring to a boil; cover, reduce heat and simmer 30 minutes. Serve with desired toppings. Makes 11 cups.

*This soup makes a lot,
so be sure to have plas-
tic containers on hand
to send everyone home
with leftover soup...if
there is any!*

White Chicken Chili
(pictured on page 104)

6 (15½-oz.) cans Great Northern
    beans, drained and rinsed
3 (5-oz.) cans chicken, drained
32-oz. container chicken broth
3 c. (12 oz.) shredded Monterey Jack
    cheese
2 (4½-oz.) cans diced green chilies

2 small onions, chopped
1½ c. sour cream
1 T. olive oil
2 t. ground cumin
1½ t. dried oregano
1 t. garlic powder
¼ t. ground white pepper

Combine all ingredients in a large stockpot. Simmer 30 minutes or until thoroughly heated. Makes 20½ cups.

Kathleen's Fabulous Chili

1 lb. ground chuck
1 lb. bacon, uncooked and chopped
1 onion, chopped
1 c. chopped green bell pepper
16-oz. can dark red kidney beans, drained
16-oz. can pinto beans, drained
15.5-oz. can Sloppy Joe mix
15-oz. can pork and beans, undrained
14.5-oz. can diced tomatoes, undrained
1 c. water
¼ c. brown sugar, packed
1 T. chili powder
½ t. salt
½ t. ground black pepper

Cook first 4 ingredients in a large skillet, stirring until beef crumbles and is no longer pink; drain.

Combine meat mixture, beans and remaining ingredients in a *6-quart slow cooker*; cover and cook on HIGH setting 4 hours. Makes 12½ cups.

"This recipe is my own creation. It won 1st place for 'Overall Best Chili' at a church chili cook-off!"

KATHY STRUNK
MESA, AZ

Farmstyle Beef Stew

1 T. vegetable shortening
3 lbs. cubed stew meat
3¾ c. water, divided
2 (14½-oz.) cans diced tomatoes
2 medium onions, vertically sliced
2 celery ribs, chopped
2 cloves garlic, minced
¼ c. chopped fresh parsley
½ t. dried thyme
1 T. salt
½ t. pepper
10 carrots, sliced (about 2 lbs.)
5 baking potatoes, cubed (about 2 lbs.)
¼ c. all-purpose flour
12 green onions, sliced (about 2 bunches)
1 c. frozen petite green peas

"I found this recipe while looking through a cupboard at my dad's house…it was even written in my late grand-mother's handwriting!"

CAROL BRASHEAR
MYERSTOWN, PA

Melt shortening over medium-high heat in a 6-quart Dutch oven. Cook meat, in batches, 6 minutes or until well browned, reserving drippings in pan. Add 2½ cups water, tomatoes and next 7 ingredients. Bring to a boil; reduce heat, cover and simmer for 1½ hours or until meat is tender, stirring occasionally.

Stir in carrots and potatoes. Bring to a boil; reduce heat, cover and simmer one hour. Gradually whisk remaining 1¼ cups water into flour. Stir flour mixture into stew; stir in green onions and peas. Bring to a boil; reduce heat and simmer, uncovered, 5 minutes or until slightly thickened, stirring often. Makes 19 cups.

It's the unexpected touches that make the biggest impressions.

When serving soup or chili, offer guests a variety of fun toppings…fill bowls with shredded cheese, oyster crackers, chopped onions, sour cream and crunchy croutons; then invite everyone to dig in!

Giant Chocolate Malt
Cookies (page 121)

For kids Only

Let your children lend a hand in the kitchen with enticing recipes like

Cheese Fries, Taco Pizza or Giant Chocolate Malt Cookies. You'll enjoy the

ease of these kid-friendly recipes while the kids enjoy the taste!

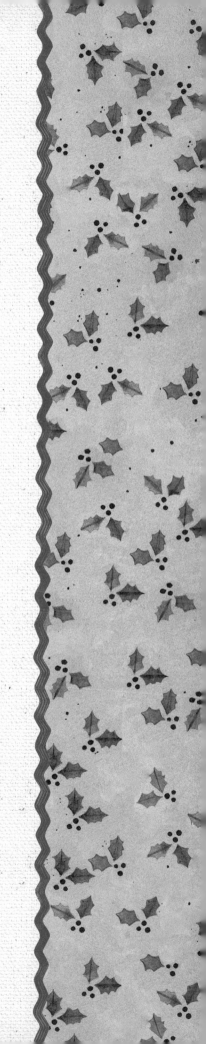

Kid's "Champagne"

1 ltr. white grape juice

2 ltrs. ginger ale

Combine ingredients and serve well chilled. Makes 12 cups.

Wake-Up Shake

1 c. milk
1 T. frozen orange juice concentrate
1 t. vanilla extract

Sugar to taste
4 to 6 ice cubes

Pour all ingredients into an electric blender; process until smooth. Serves one.

Monkey Paw Biscuits

¾ c. granulated sugar
½ t. ground cinnamon
3 (12-oz.) cans refrigerated biscuits

¼ c. evaporated milk
½ c. brown sugar, packed
¾ c. butter or margarine

Combine granulated sugar and cinnamon; set aside. Separate biscuits; cut each one into fourths. Coat biscuits with sugar and cinnamon mixture; stack in bottom and around sides of a lightly buttered 12-cup Bundt® pan.

Bring evaporated milk, brown sugar and butter to a boil in a small saucepan and cook until thickened; pour over biscuits. Bake at 350 degrees for 35 minutes; cool slightly before removing from pan. Serve warm. Serves 12.

Cheesy Chicken & Mac

3 c. diced cooked chicken
2 c. ready cut macaroni or ziti, uncooked
1¾ c. milk
2 (10¾-oz.) cans cream of chicken soup

1 c. onion, diced
8-oz. pkg. pasteurized processed cheese spread, diced
8-oz. pkg. sliced mushrooms
¼ c. dry white wine
¼ t. pepper

Mix all ingredients together in a large bowl; spoon into an ungreased 13"x9" baking dish. Refrigerate overnight. Let stand 30 minutes before baking. Bake, uncovered, at 350 degrees for 45 minutes; then cover and bake 15 more minutes. Serves 6 to 8.

Cheese Fries

32-oz. pkg. frozen French fries
1 T. chili powder
½ c. sliced green onions
½ c. crisply cooked and crumbled
   bacon (7 slices)

1 c. shredded Cheddar cheese
Ranch dressing

Leave the crumbling of the bacon to the kids, though you might want extra slices for nibbling on.

Bake fries according to package directions for crispier fries. Place baked fries in a broiler pan; sprinkle with chili powder, green onions, bacon and cheese. Broil for about 2 minutes or until cheese is melted. Serve with Ranch dressing. Serves 8.

Nachos Magnifico

Nachos Magnifico

1 lb. ground beef
1 c. chopped onion
¾ t. salt
¼ t. pepper
Tortilla chips
2 (16-oz.) cans refried beans
4.5-oz. can diced green chilies
1 c. salsa

1 c. shredded Cheddar cheese
1 c. shredded mozzarella cheese
1 c. shredded Monterey Jack cheese
12-oz. container guacamole
1½ c. sour cream
2¼-oz. can sliced black olives, drained
½ c. chopped green onions

Cook ground beef and one cup onion in a skillet, stirring until beef crumbles and is no longer pink; drain well. Add salt and pepper.

Layer tortilla chips in a lightly greased 13"x9" baking dish; top with beans, beef mixture, green chilies and salsa. Sprinkle with cheeses. Cover and bake at 400 degrees for 8 to 10 minutes or until cheese melts. Top with guacamole, sour cream, olives and green onions. Serve with additional tortilla chips. Serves 6 to 8.

For added pizzazz, use blue and yellow tortilla chips and arrange them around the edges of the dish. Let the kids sprinkle on the toppings.

Ravioli Lasagna

2 c. pasta sauce, divided
16-oz. container ricotta cheese
10-oz. pkg. frozen chopped spinach, thawed and drained
2 eggs, beaten

Salt and pepper to taste
½ c. grated Romano or Parmesan cheese
18-oz. bag frozen cheese ravioli
½ c. shredded mozzarella cheese

Spread ½ cup pasta sauce in a 5-inch deep, 8"x8" baking dish. Stir together ricotta, spinach, eggs, salt, pepper and Romano cheese in a bowl. Layer one-third of the ravioli in the baking dish; top with half the ricotta mixture. Repeat layers, ending with remaining third of ravioli. Spoon remaining pasta sauce over top; sprinkle with mozzarella.

Cover with aluminum foil and bake at 375 degrees for 40 minutes. Remove foil and continue baking 10 more minutes. Serves 4.

"A friend shared this recipe with me and it's fabulous! Prep time is short enough to make it a tasty weeknight meal."

KAREN LEE PUCHNICK
LYNDORA, PA

Spaghetti Bake

8- to 12-oz. pkg. spaghetti, cooked
2 lbs. ground beef, browned and drained
28-oz. jar spaghetti sauce

4-oz. can sliced mushrooms, drained
3 to 4 c. shredded mozzarella cheese
Grated Parmesan cheese to taste

Mix spaghetti, ground beef, sauce and mushrooms together. Spread in a greased 13"x9" baking dish; sprinkle with cheeses.

Bake, uncovered, at 350 degrees for 20 minutes or until cheese is melted. Serves 6.

"My family loves this much better than plain spaghetti…it's cheesy and delicious!"

JILL MEHRINGER
JASPER, IN

Salsa-Chippy Chicken

2 T. oil
2 T. lime juice
1 t. honey
1 lb. boneless, skinless chicken
    breasts, sliced into 1" strips

12 taco shells, crushed
16-oz. jar salsa
2 c. shredded sharp Cheddar cheese

Combine oil, lime juice and honey in a medium bowl. Dip chicken strips into oil mixture; dredge in crushed taco shells. Arrange in an ungreased 13"x9" pan and bake, uncovered, for 25 minutes or until chicken is done.

Remove chicken from oven; pour salsa over chicken and sprinkle with cheese. Bake, uncovered, 5 to 7 more minutes or until cheese is melted. Serves 4.

Cheeseburger & Fries Casserole

2 lbs. ground beef
10¾-oz. can golden mushroom soup

10¾-oz. can Cheddar cheese soup
20-oz. pkg. frozen French fries

Cook ground beef in a large skillet, stirring until it crumbles and is no longer pink; drain well. Stir in soups and pour into an ungreased 13"x9" baking dish; arrange French fries on top. Bake, uncovered, at 350 degrees for 50 to 55 minutes. Serves 6 to 8.

Taco Pizza

8-oz. pkg. corn muffin mix
1¼-oz. pkg. taco seasoning mix,
    divided
1 lb. ground beef, browned
½ c. taco sauce

1 c. shredded Cheddar cheese
Toppings: sour cream, chopped
    tomatoes, chopped green onions,
    hot peppers, salsa, shredded lettuce

Prepare corn muffin mix according to package directions; spread in a greased 8"x8" baking dish. Bake at 400 degrees for 6 to 8 minutes.

Stir ½ package of taco seasoning mix into beef, reserving remaining mix for another recipe. Add any additional ingredients according to taco seasoning mix directions, reducing each by half.

Remove cornbread from oven and spread with taco sauce. Top with beef mixture and cheese. Return to oven; continue baking 15 more minutes or until cheese is melted. Let stand 2 to 3 minutes; cut into squares. Serve with desired toppings. Serves 2 to 4.

Cinnamon Puffs

8-oz. pkg. cream cheese
1 egg yolk
½ c. plus 2 T. sugar, divided
1 t. vanilla extract

1 loaf sliced white bread, crusts
  removed
1 T. ground cinnamon
1 c. butter, melted and cooled

Beat cream cheese, egg yolk, 2 tablespoons sugar and vanilla in a medium bowl at medium speed with an electric mixer. Roll bread slices flat; spread cream cheese filling on bread. Roll up jelly roll-style. Combine remaining ½ cup sugar and cinnamon in a small bowl. Dip bread in butter and then in cinnamon-sugar mixture. Place on baking sheets and freeze. Cut each roll into 3 pieces. Bake at 350 degrees for 15 minutes. Makes 45 bite-size pieces.

Giant Chocolate Malt Cookies

(pictured on page 114)

1 c. butter-flavored shortening
1¼ c. brown sugar, packed
½ c. malted milk powder
2 T. chocolate syrup
1 T. vanilla extract
1 egg

2 c. all-purpose flour
1 t. baking soda
½ t. salt
1½ c. semi-sweet chocolate chunks
1 c. milk chocolate chips

Combine first 5 ingredients in a large mixing bowl; mix at medium speed with an electric mixer for 2 minutes. Add egg; mix well and set aside.

Stir together flour, soda and salt; add shortening mixture, mixing well. Fold in chocolate. Shape dough into ½-cup balls; press down to form 3½-inch round discs. Arrange 3 inches apart on ungreased baking sheets. Bake at 375 degrees for 15 minutes. Cool for 5 minutes; remove to a wire rack to cool completely. Makes 8 cookies.

Almond Grahams

12 whole graham crackers
1 c. butter or margarine
1 c. brown sugar, packed

½ t. vanilla extract
1 c. sliced almonds
1 c. flaked coconut

Place crackers in a greased 15"x10" jelly-roll pan; set aside. Bring butter and brown sugar to a boil in a saucepan, stirring constantly, for 2 to 3 minutes until sugar melts; add vanilla. Pour over crackers, spreading evenly. Sprinkle with sliced almonds and coconut. Bake at 400 degrees for 5 minutes; break or cut into pieces. Makes 8 cups.

Holly-Jolly
Almond Brittle
(page 132)

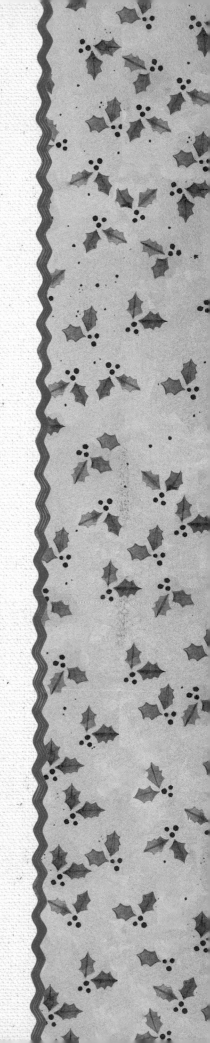

Cookie & Candy exchange

The holidays and sweet treats go hand-in-hand. For old-fashioned cookie cutouts to decadent chocolaty treats, look no further. Check out the festive gift cards on page 133 that can be copied, cut and colored to "tag" along with these holiday confection gifts.

Waffle Cookies

White Chocolate-Cranberry Cookies

18-oz. tube refrigerated white
chocolate chunk cookie dough,
softened
1 c. chopped pecans

¾ c. sweetened, dried cranberries
1 t. orange extract
1 t. vanilla extract

Combine all ingredients in a large bowl; mix well. Drop by heaping teaspoonfuls, 2 to 3 inches apart, onto ungreased baking sheets. Bake at 350 degrees for 8 to 10 minutes. Makes 2 to 3 dozen.

"Cranberries add a chewy tartness to these cookies...a tasty treat."

SANDY BERNARDS
VALENCIA, CA

Waffle Cookies

4 (1-oz.) squares unsweetened baking
chocolate
1 c. butter or margarine
1½ c. sugar

4 eggs
2 t. vanilla extract
2 c. all-purpose flour
Chocolate Frosting

Melt together chocolate and butter in a heavy saucepan over low heat; stir in sugar until dissolved. Remove from heat and whisk in eggs, vanilla and flour until blended. Drop by teaspoonfuls onto a heated waffle iron; bake according to manufacturer's instructions. Top with Chocolate Frosting. Makes 4 dozen.

Chocolate Frosting

2 (1-oz.) squares unsweetened baking
chocolate
¼ c. butter or margarine

¼ c. milk
2 t. vanilla extract
3 c. powdered sugar, sifted

Melt chocolate and butter in a heavy saucepan over low heat; remove from heat and add milk and vanilla. Mix in powdered sugar to desired consistency. Makes 1½ cups.

THERE'S NO EASIER GIFT BAG THAN A CLASSIC BROWN PAPER LUNCH SACK. Fill with treats, fold the top over, punch 2 holes and slide a peppermint stick or candy cane through. You could even thread a licorice whip through the holes and tie into a bow!

Moravian Spice Crisps

¾ c. all-purpose flour
½ t. baking powder
¼ t. baking soda
¼ t. salt
½ t. ground cinnamon
½ t. ground ginger

½ t. ground white pepper
¼ c. ground cloves
⅓ c. light brown sugar, packed
3 T. butter, softened
¼ c. light molasses

Combine flour, baking powder, soda, salt and spices; set aside. Beat brown sugar and butter in a mixing bowl at high speed with an electric mixer until creamy. Beat in molasses at medium speed until blended. Stir in flour mixture.

Drop batter by rounded teaspoonfuls about 4 inches apart on greased baking sheets; press each into a 2-inch circle. Bake at 350 degrees for 8 to 10 minutes. Let cool several minutes; remove to wire racks to cool completely. Store in a tightly covered container. Makes about 3 dozen.

Stained Glass Cookies

½ c. butter or margarine, softened
½ c. shortening
1 c. sugar
1 egg
1 t. vanilla extract

2½ c. all-purpose flour
½ t. baking soda
½ t. salt
Colored hard candies, crushed

Beat butter and shortening in a large bowl at medium speed with an electric mixer until creamy. Add sugar, egg and vanilla; beat well. Stir together flour, baking soda and salt; add to butter mixture and beat well. Form dough into a ball; wrap in wax paper and chill one to 2 hours or until firm enough to shape.

Shape dough by tablespoonfuls into 9-inch-long thin ropes; form ropes into closed shapes such as triangles, circles, hearts, bells or stars. Place shapes on parchment-lined baking sheets. Fill insides of shapes with crushed candies. Bake at 350 degrees for 10 to 12 minutes or until candy melts. Makes about 3 dozen.

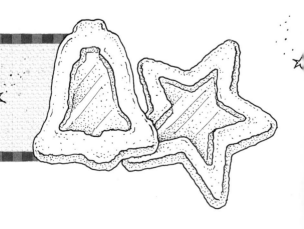

OVERLAP COOKIES IN A WREATH SHAPE and dust with powdered sugar for a snowy look. Perfect for nibbling on before the cookie exchange begins.

Chocolate Cutouts

1 egg, beaten
⅔ c. butter, softened
¾ c. granulated sugar
1½ c. all-purpose flour
¼ c. baking cocoa

1 t. baking powder
½ t. salt
1 t. vanilla extract
Optional: frosting, colored sugar

Beat egg, butter and ¾ cup granulated sugar in a mixing bowl at medium speed with an electric mixer until creamy. Stir together flour and next 4 ingredients. Add to egg mixture, beating until combined. Form dough into 2 flattened rounds; cover and chill.

Roll dough out on a floured surface to ⅛-inch thickness. Cut with cookie cutters as desired; place on ungreased baking sheets. Bake at 350 degrees for 8 to 10 minutes. Let cool; frost and sprinkle with colored sugar, if desired. Makes 2 to 3 dozen.

"You'll have a hard time eating just one!"

Nancy Cavagnaro
Mountain View, CA

Orange-You-Glad Cookies

1 c. butter, softened
1 c. sugar
1 egg, beaten
2½ c. all-purpose flour

1 t. baking powder
2 T. orange juice
1 T. vanilla extract

Combine butter, sugar and egg in a large mixing bowl; beat at medium speed with an electric mixer until creamy, about one to 2 minutes. Add flour, baking powder, orange juice and vanilla, mix one to 2 more minutes. Cover and chill for 2 to 3 hours until dough is firm.

Roll dough to ¼-inch thickness and cut into shapes with cookie cutters. Place one inch apart on lightly greased baking sheets. Bake at 350 degrees for 6 to 10 minutes until edges are lightly golden. Cool and frost. Makes 2 dozen.

"I get requests for this cookie recipe all the time!"

Jackie Balla
Walbridge, OH

Frosting

3 c. powdered sugar
⅓ c. butter, softened
1 t. vanilla extract

1 to 2 T. orange juice
Red and yellow food coloring

Combine all ingredients in a mixing bowl; beat at medium speed with an electric mixer until fluffy. Makes 1½ cups.

Holiday Gumdrop Cookies

1 c. butter, softened
1 c. sugar
2 eggs
1 t. vanilla extract
2 c. all-purpose flour
1 t. baking powder

½ t. baking soda
¼ t. salt
1 c. quick-cooking oats, uncooked
1 c. flaked coconut
1 c. pecans, coarsely chopped
1 c. gumdrops, sliced

Beat butter and sugar at medium speed with an electric mixer until creamy. Stir in eggs, one at a time, and vanilla until well mixed; set aside. Stir together flour, baking powder, soda and salt; add to butter mixture and mix well. Stir in oats and remaining ingredients just until mixed; refrigerate dough 30 minutes.

With floured hands, roll dough into 1½-inch balls and flatten slightly; place on parchment paper-lined baking sheets. Bake at 375 degrees for 13 minutes. Makes about 2 dozen.

Chocolate Snowballs

2 c. granulated sugar
½ c. milk
¾ c. butter or margarine
6 T. baking cocoa

3 c. quick-cooking oats, uncooked
1 c. chopped pecans
1 t. vanilla extract
Garnish: powdered sugar

Combine granulated sugar, milk, butter and cocoa in a saucepan. Bring to a boil over medium heat, stirring constantly. When mixture comes to a boil, remove from heat; stir in oats, pecans and vanilla. Allow to cool to room temperature.

Shape into one-inch balls; roll in powdered sugar. Keep refrigerated in an airtight container. Makes about 3 dozen.

Can't-Leave-Alone Bars

18¼-oz. pkg. white cake mix
2 eggs
⅓ c. oil

14-oz. can sweetened condensed milk
6-oz. pkg. semi-sweet chocolate chips
¼ c. butter, sliced

Combine cake mix, eggs and oil in a bowl; mix well. With floured hands, press two-thirds of mixture into a greased 13"x9" pan. Set aside.

Combine condensed milk, chocolate chips and butter in a microwave-safe bowl. Microwave, uncovered, on HIGH (100%) for 45 seconds. Stir and microwave 45 to 60 more seconds or until chips and butter are melted. Stir until smooth; pour over cake mixture in pan. Drop remaining cake mixture by teaspoonfuls over top. Bake at 350 degrees for 20 to 25 minutes or until light golden. Let cool before cutting into squares. Makes 3 dozen.

Peanutty Caramel Bars

14-oz. pkg. caramels, unwrapped
¼ c. water
¾ c. creamy peanut butter, divided
4 c. doughnut-shaped oat cereal

1 c. peanuts
1 c. milk chocolate chips
½ c. butter, melted

Heat caramels, water and ½ cup peanut butter in a large saucepan until melted. Add cereal and peanuts; stir until coated. Spread into a greased 13"x9" pan; set aside.

Heat chocolate chips, butter and remaining ¼ cup peanut butter in another pan over low heat until melted; spread over cereal mixture. Refrigerate before cutting into bars. Makes about 3 dozen.

"Nothing says holidays more than trays filled with cookies that have been made with love in your own kitchen!"

SHEILA PLACKE
CARROLLTON, MO

Mint Brownies

19½-oz. pkg. fudge brownie mix
3-oz. pkg. cream cheese, softened
½ c. butter, softened
1 T. milk

½ t. peppermint extract
3 or 4 drops green food coloring
2 c. powdered sugar
Garnish: chocolate frosting

Prepare brownies according to package directions, using the amount of eggs for cake-like brownies. Bake in a greased 13"x9" pan according to package directions. Let cool.

Mix cream cheese and butter in a bowl until creamy. Add milk, peppermint extract, food coloring and powdered sugar. Spread on cooled brownies; let mint layer harden. Spread with chocolate frosting; cut into squares. Makes 2½ to 3 dozen.

"When I make these for my husband, I usually end up getting only a small square…they go fast!"

BETH POWELL
POTOSI, WI

Gooseberry Patch
Delaware, OH

To: Kris K.
Winter Ln.
North Pole

MAILING COOKIES IS A SNAP… JUST FOLLOW THESE POINTERS. Choose firm cookies such as sliced, drop or bar cookies; avoid frosted or filled ones. Line a sturdy box with plastic bubble wrap and pack cookies in a single layer with wax paper between the layers.

Peanut Butter–Cocoa Truffles

¾ c. butter
1 c. peanut butter chips
½ c. baking cocoa
14-oz. can sweetened condensed milk

1 T. vanilla extract
Garnish: baking cocoa, finely chopped
    nuts, graham cracker crumbs

Combine first 4 ingredients in a large saucepan over low heat. Stir constantly until mixture is thick and glossy, about 9 minutes. Remove from heat; stir in vanilla. Chill for 4 hours or until firm enough to handle.

Shape into one-inch balls; roll in cocoa, nuts or crumbs. Chill until firm, about one hour. Store, covered, in the refrigerator. Makes about 3 dozen.

Chocolate–Coconut Bonbons

2 (1-oz.) squares unsweetened baking
    chocolate
14-oz. can sweetened condensed milk

2 c. flaked coconut, packed
½ c. chopped walnuts

Melt chocolate over low heat in a heavy saucepan. Remove from heat and stir in condensed milk and remaining ingredients. Drop by teaspoonfuls onto greased baking sheets, shaping with hands into balls.

Preheat oven to 350 degrees; turn off heat. Place baking sheets in oven for 20 minutes. Remove from oven and let cookies cool completely on baking sheets. Makes about 6 dozen.

ONE OF MY FAVORITE MEMORIES involves creating a holiday treat with my then 4-year-old daughter, Raisa. I decided that my daughter and I should attempt to create a gingerbread house. Knowing my creative limitations, I opted for a "pre-fab" kit. After several attempts, we managed to get the house (which looked more like a shanty) to stand. My daughter then began to decorate with pounds of gumdrops, peppermints, licorice sticks, wafers and candies. By the time we finished, it looked like a joke…frosting everywhere, candies scattered and the house looked like it would collapse if you stared at it too long. I was about ready to toss the whole mess out when my daughter whispered, "Isn't it the prettiest house you've ever seen? And we made it!" Nobody would ever suggest that our gingerbread house would win any blue ribbons, but to my daughter it was a glorious achievement. And what she taught me that year was that it was the effort and time we spent together that was important…not whether or not the gumdrops were lined up in a perfect row.

Valerie Orleans
Anaheim Hills, CA

Peanut Butter-
Cocoa Truffles

Holly-Jolly Almond Brittle

(pictured on page 122)

2 c. sugar
½ c. water

6 T. butter, melted
2 c. whole almonds

Butter a large baking sheet; set aside.

Combine sugar and water in a 3-quart heavy saucepan. Bring to a boil, stirring gently to dissolve sugar. Wash down crystals on sides of pan with a small brush dipped in hot water. Insert a candy thermometer. Bring mixture to a boil over medium-high heat; cook until thermometer reaches 280 degrees, washing down crystals occasionally.

Reduce heat to medium; stir in butter and almonds. Mixture will crystallize, but continue to cook until mixture melts and thermometer registers 306 degrees, stirring often to blend melting sugar with crystallized sugar. Quickly pour mixture onto prepared baking sheet. Let cool. When hardened, break into pieces. Store at room temperature in an airtight container. Makes about 1½ pounds.

Meringue Kisses

3 egg whites
¼ t. cream of tartar
⅔ c. sugar

½ t. peppermint extract
¼ t. green liquid food coloring
½ c. semi-sweet chocolate mini chips

Beat egg whites at high speed with an electric mixer until foamy; beat in cream of tartar. Slowly beat in sugar, one tablespoon at a time, until sugar dissolves and stiff peaks form. Beat in peppermint extract and food coloring; fold in chocolate chips. Drop mixture by teaspoonfuls onto parchment paper-lined baking sheets.

Bake at 250 degrees for 45 minutes; turn off oven and leave overnight. Store in an airtight container at room temperature. Makes 4 dozen.

For Snowman-shaped Meringues:

Spoon meringue into a gallon-size heavy-duty zip-top plastic bag. Snip off one corner to get a ¾-inch opening. Pipe 2 circles (one bigger than the other); flatten with a spatula, if necessary. Decorate with additional candies as desired. Bake as directed. Makes 3 dozen.

To:
Let us eat Cookies!
From:

Include these festive tags with your merry treats. Just copy, cut and color!

Baked with LOVE
From the Kitchen of:

Candy Bar Fudge

½ c. butter
⅓ c. baking cocoa
¼ c. brown sugar, packed
¼ c. milk
3¾ c. powdered sugar
1 t. vanilla extract

30 caramels, unwrapped
2 T. water
2 c. salted peanuts
¾ c. milk chocolate chips
¾ c. butterscotch chips

"I hope you enjoy this recipe that I hold dear to my heart."

LORI BRANDES
WELLSVILLE, NY

Combine butter, cocoa, brown sugar and milk in a large microwave-safe bowl. Microwave on HIGH (100%) one minute; stir well. Continue to microwave on HIGH 2 more minutes or until mixture comes to a boil. Gradually stir in powdered sugar and vanilla. Press into a lightly greased 8"x8" pan; set aside.

Combine caramels and water in another microwave-safe bowl; microwave on HIGH 2 to 3 minutes or until melted and bubbling. Pour evenly over cocoa layer in pan; sprinkle with peanuts.

Combine milk chocolate chips and butterscotch chips in another medium-size microwave-safe bowl; microwave on HIGH one to 2 minutes or until melted. Spread evenly over peanut layer in pan. Chill until firm; let stand 15 to 20 minutes at room temperature before cutting into squares. Makes 3 pounds.

Nana's Christmas
Caramels (page 145)

Giftable goodies

Delight your loved ones with these heartfelt gifts from the kitchen.

We've included whimsical labels with the recipes' preparation directions that

you can copy and attach to many of the mixes like Ginger & Spice &

Everything Nice Muffin Mix. You'll also find creative packing ideas such as

shaping Marvelous Mocha Fudge in mini Bundt® pans and wrapping the little

pans in clear cellophane. Be inspired and share in the spirit of the season.

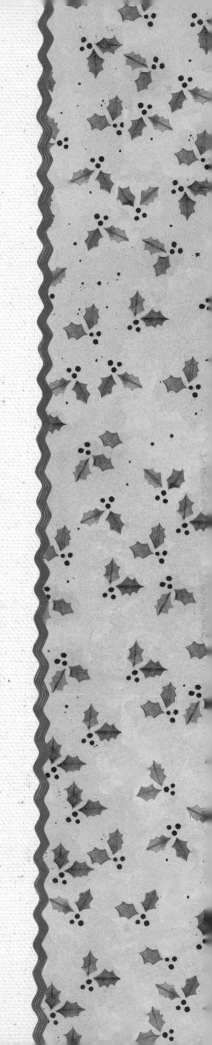

Munch & Crunch
Snack Mix

Munch & Crunch Snack Mix

This crunchy snack has a southwestern kick!

1 c. mini pretzels
1 c. corn chips
1 c. oyster crackers
1 c. roasted, salted pumpkin seed kernels
1 c. honey-roasted peanuts
2 T. butter or margarine, melted

2 T. brown sugar, packed
1 t. chili powder
1 t. Worcestershire sauce
½ t. onion salt
½ t. ground cumin
⅛ t. ground red pepper

Toss together first 5 ingredients in a large bowl; set aside. Whisk together butter and remaining 6 ingredients in another bowl; pour over snack mix, stirring to coat. Spread mix in a roasting pan; bake at 300 degrees for 25 minutes, stirring after 12 minutes. Cool completely; store in an airtight container. Makes about 5 cups.

Cup of Veggie Noodle Soup Mix

⅓ c. dried mixed vegetable flakes
1 T. cracked wheat
2 T. angel hair pasta, coarsely broken and uncooked
¼ t. dried parsley

⅛ t. dried, minced onion
¼ t. dried basil
⅛ t. garlic powder
⅛ t. onion powder

Process dried mixed vegetables in an electric blender or a food processor until pea-size flakes form; place in a bowl. Add cracked wheat and remaining ingredients; toss to mix well. Divide and place into 2 plastic zip-lock bags; press to make as airtight as possible. Attach instructions. Makes 2 mixes.

Instructions

Pour one package soup mix into a bowl or large mug; pour one cup boiling water, chicken broth or beef broth over soup mix. Stir to mix. Makes one serving.

Make a copy of this label to attach to the soup mix.

Cup of **VEGGIE NOODLE** Soup Mix

Pour one package soup mix into a bowl or large mug; pour one cup boiling water, chicken broth or beef broth on top. Stir to mix. Makes 1 serving.

Ginger & Spice & Everything Nice
Muffin Mix

1¾ c. all-purpose flour
½ c. sugar
1 T. baking powder
¼ t. baking soda
1 t. vanilla powder

2 t. ground cinnamon
½ t. ground nutmeg
1 t. ground ginger
⅛ t. ground cloves
¼ t. salt

Stir together all ingredients in a bowl; place in an airtight container. Attach instructions. Makes 2 cups.

Instructions

Combine muffin mix with ½ cup melted butter, one egg and one cup milk; stir just until moistened. Fill greased or paper-lined muffin cups ⅔ full with batter; bake at 400 degrees for 15 minutes. Makes one dozen.

Don't forget to include a colored copy of the label to attach with the muffin mix!

Ginger & Spice & Everything Nice MUFFIN MIX

Combine muffin mix with ½ cup melted butter, 1 egg and 1 cup milk; stir until just moistened. Fill greased or paper-lined muffin tins ⅔ full of batter; bake at 400° for 15 minutes. Makes 12.

On the gift tag:

Ginger & Spice & Everything Nice

MUFFIN MIX

Combine muffin mix with ½ cup melted butter, 1 egg, and 1 cup milk; stir until just moistened. Fill greased or paper-lined muffin tins ⅔ full of batter. Bake at 400° for 15 minutes. Makes 12.

Gotta-Have-It Cornbread Mix

6 c. all-purpose flour
6 c. cornmeal
2 c. powdered milk
1 c. sugar

⅓ c. baking powder
1 T. salt
1½ c. shortening

Combine first 6 ingredients together in a large bowl; cut in shortening with a pastry blender or 2 forks until mixture resembles coarse crumbs. Store in an airtight container at room temperature for up to 6 weeks or freeze for up to 6 months. Attach instructions. Makes 16 cups.

Instructions

Combine 2 cups cornbread mix with one teaspoon chili powder in a large mixing bowl; form a well in the center and set aside. Whisk one egg and ¾ cup water together; pour into well. Mix just until combined; spread batter in a greased 8"x8" pan. Bake at 425 degrees for 20 to 25 minutes or until a toothpick inserted in the center comes out clean. Makes 16 servings.

Package Gotta-Have-It Cornbread Mix with a mini cornstick pan and a jar of salsa. Add a line to instructions: "For a quick & easy appetizer, bake batter in pan, then dip tiny cornsticks into salsa." Delicious!

Tuxedo Brownies in a Jar

½ c. walnuts
½ c. white chocolate chips
½ c. semi-sweet chocolate chips
⅔ c. brown sugar, packed

1 c. plus 2 T. all-purpose flour
⅓ c. baking cocoa
⅔ c. granulated sugar
½ t. salt

Layer all ingredients in order listed in a one-quart, wide-mouth jar, being sure to pack down after each addition. Secure lid and attach baking instructions and a gift tag. Makes about 4 cups.

Instructions

Empty brownie mix into a large bowl. Add 3 eggs, ½ cup oil and one teaspoon vanilla extract. Pour into a greased 9"x9" pan. Bake at 350 degrees for 22 to 25 minutes. Cut into squares. Serves 6 to 8.

Praline Ice Cream Syrup

Make hand-dipped waffle cones to give with Praline Ice Cream Syrup. Dip the top half of cones in melted chocolate chips, then roll in chopped peanuts or colorful sprinkles.

2 c. corn syrup
⅓ c. brown sugar, packed
½ c. water
1¼ c. chopped pecans

½ t. vanilla extract
4 (1-pt.) canning jars and lids, sterilized

Combine syrup, sugar and water in a saucepan. Bring to a boil over medium heat; boil for one minute. Remove from heat; stir in pecans and vanilla.

Pour into hot jars, leaving ¼-inch space at the top. Secure lids; process in a boiling water bath for 10 minutes. Makes 4 pints.

Lotsa Pepper Jelly

"Attach a festive card to each jar with serving suggestions such as: Spoon over cream cheese-topped crackers or use as a glaze on roast turkey or ham."

TERESA HILL
LIMA, NY

2 large green bell peppers, seeded and cut into 2" pieces
4 large jalapeño peppers, halved crosswise
1 c. cider vinegar

6 c. sugar
2 (3-oz.) pkgs. liquid pectin
7 (½-pt.) canning jars and lids, sterilized

Process peppers in a food processor until liquefied; pour into a 6-quart Dutch oven. Stir in vinegar and sugar. Bring mixture to a boil, stirring constantly. Add pectin and stir until well blended. Return mixture to a boil and boil for one minute. Remove from heat and skim off foam.

Pour into hot jars, leaving ¼-inch space at the top. Secure lids; process in a boiling water bath for 5 minutes. Makes 7 (8-ounce) jars.

Tuxedo Brownies
in a Jar

Almond-Pear Muffins

1¼ c. all-purpose flour
¾ c. brown sugar, packed
1 T. baking powder
1 t. ground ginger, divided
½ t. salt
1 c. chopped pears
1 c. whole-bran cereal

1 c. milk
1 egg
¼ c. oil
2 T. chopped almonds
8-oz. pkg. cream cheese, softened
1 T. honey

Combine flour, brown sugar, baking powder, ½ teaspoon ginger and salt in a large bowl; stir in pears and set aside. Mix cereal and milk together; set aside for 5 minutes.

Add egg and oil to cereal mixture; mix into pear mixture just until moistened. Fill greased or paper-lined muffin cups ¾ full with batter; sprinkle tops with almonds. Bake at 400 degrees for 18 to 20 minutes; cool.

Mix together cream cheese, honey and remaining ½ teaspoon ginger; serve with muffins as a spread. Serves 12 to 16.

Chocolate-Covered Peanut Clusters

2 (12-oz.) pkgs. semi-sweet chocolate chips
1 c. creamy peanut butter

16-oz. pkg. mini marshmallows
2½ c. milk chocolate-covered peanuts
Powdered sugar

Melt chocolate chips with peanut butter in a heavy saucepan; stir until smooth. Remove from heat; stir in marshmallows and chocolate-covered peanuts. Drop by tablespoonfuls onto a wax paper-lined baking sheet. Chill until firm; sprinkle with powdered sugar before serving. Makes about 4 dozen.

Candied Nuts

½ lb. whole nuts, shelled and halved
1 egg white
1 t. water
½ lb. nuts, finely ground

½ c. sugar
½ t. ground cinnamon
½ t. salt

Place halved nuts on a lightly greased baking sheet; set aside. Beat together egg white and water; pour over halved nuts and stir to coat well. Combine ground nuts, sugar, cinnamon and salt; sprinkle over coated nuts; mix well. Bake at 200 degrees for one hour, stirring every 15 minutes. Makes about one pound.

Sugared Pecans

1 c. sugar
1½ t. salt
1 t. ground cinnamon

1 egg white
1 T. water
1-lb. pkg. pecan halves

Combine first 3 ingredients in a small bowl; set aside. Whisk egg white and water together until frothy; fold in pecan halves. Add sugar mixture; stir to coat pecans. Spread on an aluminum foil-lined baking sheet; bake at 300 degrees for 30 to 35 minutes. Remove from oven; separate pecans using a fork as they cool. Store in an airtight container. Makes about one pound.

Make a batch of these for yourself to munch on while wrapping gifts.

Chocolate Pretzels

¾ c. butter, softened
¾ c. sugar
1 egg
1 t. vanilla extract
2 c. all-purpose flour

⅓ c. baking cocoa
2 t. baking powder
¼ t. salt
Garnish: assorted sprinkles or finely chopped nuts

Beat butter and sugar at medium speed with an electric mixer until light and fluffy. Add egg and vanilla; beat well. Add flour, cocoa, baking powder and salt; beat at low speed just until blended.

Divide dough in half. Wrap one half in plastic wrap; set aside. Shape remaining dough by tablespoonfuls into 9-inch-long ropes. Twist into pretzel shapes; lightly press into sprinkles or nuts. Arrange cookies, sprinkle-side up, on lightly greased baking sheets; repeat with remaining dough. Bake at 350 degrees for 12 minutes or until set; remove to wire rack to cool completely. Makes about 2 dozen.

Easy as A-B-C! Instead of shaping Chocolate Pretzels into traditional pretzel shapes, form dough into letters... spell out names, "Joy" or "Celebrate."

Fabulous Festive Candy

10-oz. pkg. mini pretzels
5 c. doughnut-shaped oat cereal
5 c. bite-size crispy corn cereal
squares
2 c. salted peanuts
16-oz. pkg. candy-coated chocolates
2 (12-oz.) pkgs. white chocolate chips
3 T. vegetable oil

Combine pretzels, cereals, peanuts and candy-coated chocolates in a large bowl; set aside. Place chocolate chips and oil in a microwave-safe bowl; microwave on HIGH (100%) for 1½ minutes, stirring halfway through cooking time. Stir chocolate until smooth; pour over pretzel mixture and mix well. Spread onto wax paper-lined baking sheets. Let cool; break apart. Store in an airtight container. Makes 20 cups.

Marvelous Mocha Fudge

1½ c. sugar
⅔ c. evaporated milk
3 T. instant coffee granules
2 T. butter
¼ t. salt
2 c. mini marshmallows
2 c. semi-sweet chocolate chips
1 t. vanilla extract
½ t. ground cinnamon

Combine first 5 ingredients in a heavy saucepan; bring to a boil over medium heat, stirring constantly. Boil, stirring constantly, for 4 to 5 minutes; remove from heat. Mix in marshmallows and remaining ingredients; stir until marshmallows are melted. Pour into an aluminum foil-lined 8"x8" baking pan; chill 2 to 3 hours or until firm. Lift fudge from pan; remove foil and cut into squares. Makes 4 to 5 dozen.

Need to make a few gifts in a jiffy?

Whip up a batch of Marvelous Mocha Fudge and pour it into mini Bundt® pans. Wrap each in cellophane, tie with a ribbon and tuck a butter knife into the bow.

Here Come the Fudge

Christmas Wreath Cookies

1¾ c. all-purpose flour
1½ t. baking powder
½ t. salt
½ c. shortening
1 c. granulated sugar
1 egg

¾ t. vanilla extract
¼ t. almond extract
¼ c. chopped blanched almonds
1 egg white, beaten
Green decorating sugar
Red cinnamon candies

Stir together flour, baking powder and salt; set aside. Beat shortening at medium speed with an electric mixer until creamy. Gradually add one cup sugar, beating until fluffy. Blend in egg and flavorings; fold in almonds. Stir in dry ingredients; cover and chill for 3 hours.

Divide dough in half and roll out each half between 2 sheets of wax paper to ⅛-inch thickness. Cut out cookies with a leaf-shape cutter. Arrange leaves in groups of 2 or 3 on an ungreased baking sheet; brush surfaces with egg white. Sprinkle cookies with green sugar and place 3 or 4 cinnamon candies at the base of the leaves. Bake at 375 degrees for 8 to 10 minutes. Cool on wire racks. Makes 3 dozen.

Nana's Christmas Caramels

(pictured on page 134)

1 c. butter
1 c. milk
1 c. whipping cream
2 c. granulated sugar

1 c. brown sugar, packed
1 c. light corn syrup
1 t. vanilla extract

Grease around the inside top of a Dutch oven to prevent boiling over.

Melt butter in Dutch oven; use a brush and some of the melted butter to grease a heavy-duty foil-lined 9"x9" pan; set aside.

Add milk and next 4 ingredients to Dutch oven. Cook, stirring constantly, over medium-high heat 35 to 38 minutes until mixture reaches firm-ball stage (250 degrees). Remove from heat and stir in vanilla. Quickly pour caramel into prepared pan. Let stand at room temperature or in the refrigerator until firm.

Lift out caramel and invert onto a cutting board; remove foil. Cut into 1"x1" squares; wrap each square with wax paper and twist ends. Makes about 2½ lbs.

"There was a special time of excitement and anticipation in our house back in the 1950s when our grandmother made Christmas candy. It would be a cold, snowy day and my brothers and I were thrilled with these yummy caramels. We could always count on getting them in our Christmas stockings!"

JUDI TOWNER
TOWANDA, PA

Special Section: Holiday

Flip through these pages for helpful hints throughout the holidays. You'll find ideas for seasonal projects, luscious menus, party planning and even journaling suggestions for capturing your memorable events.

Holiday Hints...

For Decorating

- **Turn cookies into yummy edible place markers;** just use frosting to write each guest's name.
- **For a sweet topiary, slide a candy cane stick into the center of a foam ball,** and then cover the ball with peppermint candies. Secure the candy stick in a festive terra-cotta pot filled with florist foam.
- **For a clever and festive tablecloth, cover a table with giftwrap.**
- **Add whimsy to windows** by tying a pine cone onto each end of a ribbon for festive curtain tiebacks.
- **Dress up your mantel** with chunky scented candles that are tied with homespun or sheer ribbon. Arrange the candles among fruit and greenery.
- **Add sparkle to your centerpiece** by using sugared fruit. Brush apples, pears and plums with a thin mixture of meringue powder and water, roll in coarse sugar and let dry.
- **Serve holiday snacks & treats on a peppermint stick tray!** Cut a piece of cardboard into the desired tray size and cover with peppermint sticks using royal icing as the "glue." Allow to harden overnight before use.
- **For tree skirts, use old quilts and blankets from your children's nursery.** Just wrap around the bottom of the tree and you'll have a nostalgic, country touch in no time.

From Gooseberry Patch Crafters

Recipe Magnets

Last Christmas I made ceramic tile recipe magnets for my friends & family. I chose my favorite homestyle recipes, typed them on the computer so they would fit on the tiles and printed them out on decorative paper. I then decoupaged the recipes to square tiles, took them to a well-ventilated area and sprayed each tile with a coat of clear sealer. Once the sealer was dry, I hot-glued a heavy-duty magnet to the back of each tile. Everyone was so happy to get these as gifts because I usually make these tried & true recipes for them once a year...now they can make them whenever they want!

Maile Helekahi, Honolulu, HI

Jar of Thank-You's

A couple of years ago, I gave my mom a "jar of thank-you's." I decorated a glass canning jar with stickers and ribbons and then filled it with about 100 strips of paper on which I had thanked my mom for all the little things she did to make my life so wonderful. I included things like "Making orange juice Popsicles for me and my friends," "Letting me have slumber parties," "Making snickerdoodles," "Encouraging me when I was away at college," and "Adjusting my veil on my wedding day." Christmas morning, she read a few aloud and was so moved that she saved the rest to read on her own. She told me later that it was the best gift I had ever given her.

Michelle Kirk, Hampton, VA

Guide

For Gifts

- **Keep your eyes open year-round at tag sales and flea markets** for anything that you might be able to tuck your holiday sweets into. Vintage pie tins, mugs, jelly jars or enamelware pails would all be perfect!

- **Give neighbors a cookie kit.** Fill a basket or holiday tin with ready-made dough, sprinkles, cookie cutters, frosting and a favorite recipe.

- **Package holiday treats** such as fudge, almond brittle, cookies or brownies, in airtight containers, and then slip them into gift bags tied with ribbon or raffia. Set them in a basket by your door so there will always be a treat waiting for guests to take home.

- **Give a pail of fun!** Fill an enamelware pail with packets of hot cocoa mix, homemade cookies, bags of microwave popcorn and a classic holiday movie.

- **Be creative when giving holiday gift mixes!** Flavored coffees and teas can be given in a one-of-a-kind teacup; cocoa mix in a nostalgic milk bottle; bread mixes in an ovenproof bread crock; and soup mixes in a speckled stockpot.

- **For a personal gift tag,** string fresh cranberries on wire and shape into the recipient's initial.

- **Purchase holiday cookie cutters and make several batches of fudge in pans the depth of the cookie cutters.** Then cut out the fudge, leaving it inside the cutters, decorate with nuts, cherries or peppermints, if desired, and wrap in transparent gift bags tied with holiday ribbon.

For Kids

- **Count down the 12 Days of Christmas** by baking and decorating 12 different cookies! Slip each one in a plastic bag for each member of the family to enjoy each day.

- **Kids will love finding treats inside old-fashioned paper crackers.** Just fill a cardboard tube with candy and confetti, wrap in tissue paper and secure the ends with ribbon.

- **Pile children's toys in a wagon,** sit the toys under the tree or arrange them on a mantel for a warm-hearted, sentimental way to decorate.

- **Hang cheery mittens or Santa hats on the mantel** instead of stockings.

- **Make a mitten wreath out of mittens your children have outgrown.** Attach them to a greenery wreath and add a big bow.

- **Let the kids help make personalized giftwrap.** Just ask them to cut pictures of flowers, animals and holiday images from magazines, and then glue the images onto packages that have been wrapped in solid-color paper.

- **Trace your childrens' hands on heavy paper** to make charming gift tags.

- **If you're traveling for the holidays,** have the little ones leave Santa a note telling him where you'll be the night before Christmas!

12 Days of Christmas Menus

These menus are based on recipes found within the book.

Recipe Key: *Double recipe **Triple recipe

1

Appetizer Open House

Serves 12

*Smoky Nuts, page 89

Cheery Cheese Ring, page 20

Black-Eyed Pea Dip, page 11

Crab Rangoon, page 93

Hot Antipasto Squares, page 90

**Grapefruit Margaritas, page 85

2

Just for the Kids

Serves 8

Cheddar Fondue, page 86

Chicken Fingers with Apple Butter Peanut Sauce, page 92

Cheese Fries, page 117

Giant-Chocolate Malt Cookies, page 121

sodas and milk

3

Easy Weeknight Supper

Serves 4 to 6

Jambalaya, page 44

green salad

French bread

7

Holiday Dessert Party

Serves 16

Espresso Biscotti, page 15

Date-Nut Dessert Cheese, page 58

Chocolate-Peanut Butter Fudge, page 49

Spiced Eggnog Pound Cake, page 68

**Cranberry Hot Toddies, page 84

coffee

8

Rise & Shine Breakfast

Serves 4

Blueberry-Croissant French Toast, page 99

Crispy Brown Sugar Bacon, page 100

orange juice

9

Christmas Eve Dinner

Serves 6

Christmas Eve Oyster-Corn Chowder, page 109

Cumin Pork Roast with Wild Mushroom Sauce, page 32

Macaroni au Gratin, page 37

*Roasted Asparagus, page 46

dinner rolls

Chocolate Pecan Pie, page 39

Party Planner

Use this chart to coordinate menu items for your holiday celebration,
as well as a reminder of who's bringing what.

guests	what they're bringing (appetizer, beverage, bread, main dish, side dish, dessert)	serving pieces needed

Party Guest List

Pantry List

Party To-Do List

Holiday Memories

Remember the best parts of the holidays by jotting down your family's highlights on these pages.

Treasured Traditions

Write your family's favorite holiday traditions on these lines.

Special Holiday Activities

List events you attended this year and the ones you want to check out for next year.

Holiday Visits and Visitors

Record special visitors, houseguests and news updates from friends & family on these lines.

....

....

....

....

....

....

....

....

....

....

....

....

....

....

....

....

....

Favorite Recipes

Appetizers & Snacks ....

Beverages ....

Breakfast Entrées ....

Cakes ....

Casserole ....

Condiments ....

Cookies & Candies ....

Desserts ....

Entrées ....

Food Gifts ....

Pies & Pastries ....

Salads & Side Dishes ....

Soups & Stews ....

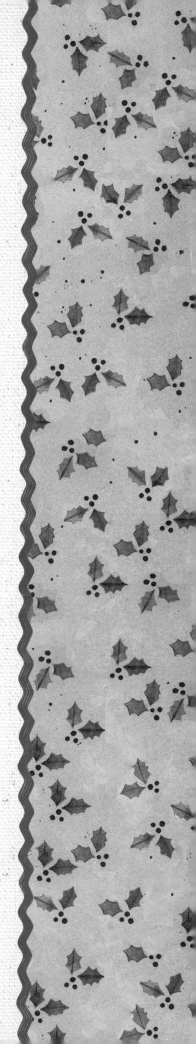

November

Copy and fill in the current year's dates. Then jot down all the events during the holiday season.

Sunday	Monday	Tuesday	Wednesday

Thursday

Friday

Saturday

December

Copy and fill in the current year's dates. Then jot down all the events during the holiday season.

Sunday	Monday	Tuesday	Wednesday

Thursday   Friday   Saturday

Recipe Index

How Did Gooseberry Patch Get Started?

You may know the story of Gooseberry Patch...the tale of two country friends who decided one day over the backyard fence to try their hands at the mail order business. Started in JoAnn's kitchen back in 1984, Vickie & JoAnn's dream of a "Country Store in Your Mailbox" has grown and grown to a 96-page catalog with over 400 products, including cookie cutters, Santas, snowmen, gift baskets, angels and our very own line of cookbooks! What an adventure for two country friends!

Through our catalogs and books, Gooseberry Patch has met country friends from all over the world. While sharing letters and phone calls, we found that our friends love to cook, decorate, garden and craft. We've created Kate, Holly & Mary Elizabeth to represent these devoted friends who live and love the country lifestyle the way we do. They're just like you & me... they're our "Country Friends®!"

Your friends at Gooseberry Patch